BURN THE

S

IMPORTANT

- The intention of this book is to inspire, entertain and educate. The opinions expressed within this book are solely the opinions of the author.

- This book is not intended as a substitute for the medical advice of a doctor or psychotherapist. Every reader is different and may therefore have different needs.

- A professional should always be consulted in matters relating to mental health and wellbeing particularly with respect to any symptoms that may require diagnosis or professional attention.

- In the event that you decide to set fire to any paper as result of reading this book please ensure that you do so in a safe and correct manner. Make sure that this is done with

|

suitable provisions to hand to extinguish any fire and steps are made to safeguard any items other than the paper from being damaged in any way.

- Inferno Books, Stephen Doran and/or any of his affiliate companies will not be held liable for any damage or harm that occurs as a result of lighting a fire and responsibility is solely on you the reader.

- We strongly recommend that if you are planning to set a fire that you do not do so alone.

- **By continuing to read on from this point you are agreeing to accept all of the above.**

BURN THE BULL SH!T

HOW TO LIVE BEFORE YOU DIE

Stephen Doran

www.burnthebullshit.com

INFERNO BOOKS

Published in the United Kingdom by:

Inferno Books

Content copyright © Stephen Doran, 2016

Illustrations copyright © Stephen Doran, 2016

Editors: Steven Baguley, Cesca Baguley

Photographs courtesy of Lucas Ambrosio Photography

A CIP record is of the book is available from the British Library

First printed January 2016

ISBN 978-0-9935128-0-3

DEDICATION

I DEDICATE THIS BOOK TO YOU AND TO A WORLD
INFLUENCED BY EVEN YOUR SMALLEST DECISIONS.
THANKS FOR BEING YOU. I HOPE YOU ENJOY READING
THIS BOOK AS MUCH AS I ENJOYED WRITING IT.

Acknowledgements

I would firstly like to thank Cesca Baguley not only for her vision and assistance in the creation of the book but more importantly for her ongoing friendship. I would like to thank my family, of course: Brian, Elisabeth and Colin. My life would not have been the joyful path to discovery without you.

I would like to extend an exceptionally large thank you to my life partner Lucy. A paragraph could never encapsulate all that you have done in supporting me on my journey so I will keep it simple. You have taught me true value and I shall be forever indebted to you. May our love continue to burn bright and fierce like the pages of this book.

I would like to thank Daniel Movahedi and Danielle Scully for being the best friends any person could ever ask for – I am truly blessed to have met you both and I am grateful for everything you have done for me. I'll always remember that you were there through the tough times and it's my honour for you to be the first to accompany me into the brighter future.

Finally, I would like to thank all of those throughout my life who have believed in me (sometimes before even I believed in myself). Whether you are reading this or not I would like to give thanks for the choices you have helped me to see. It would be impossible to say just how many of you have helped give shape or form to the information laid out in the following pages, and I am not ignorant enough to think the following chapters contain ideas that I alone have developed from scratch.

This book is merely a compilation of the ideas, concepts and discoveries that have worked for me – and can for you.

Contents

READY TO LEARN?

YOU ARE NEVER TOO OLD TO LEARN.

IN 2004, KIMANI MARUGE ENROLLED
IN THE FIRST GRADE AT 84 YEARS OLD.

Preface

If I could reach out of this book and shake your hand, I would. Actually, I'd high five you.

You are a **doer**, one of the rare few in the world that **does** – even just by picking up this book. Let's face it, regardless of where you are in life we all want better. To be better, to do better and to have better. The difference, then, is what you are willing to **do** about it.

And here you are, book in hand, ready to make it happen. The world needs more people like you. I hope to one day meet with you, have the opportunity to hear about your journey and give you a massive thanks for supporting me on mine by reading this book.

Foreword by Brad Burton

More and more I started hearing this name.

Stephen Doran, this.
Stephen Doran, that.

All over my social media…

I had to meet him.

Then one day by pure chance I'm staying in a hotel in central London and when I go down for breakfast he's sat there. The same guy who I'd been following on social media is sat at a table on his own.

Fate? Or maybe just life. *Each day presents us all with opportunities, whether or not we choose to see or take them.*

I introduced myself. He invited me to join him for breakfast.

Over the next 90 minutes we talked about everything from business, to life, to future and instantly hit it off.

It was quite clear to me that his upbringing and time as a firefighter had been incredibly important in shaping Steve both professionally and personally. He moved fast as in his old world speed was key. His actions and decisions resulted in the saving of lives. He still saves lives now, just in a different context, with his words and teachings.

That's what this book is about. An extension of his influence, which starts with you understanding that your own mindset, your own decisions dictate whether you win or lose in any area of your life.

I found myself watching a programme on the BBC, Special Forces: Ultimate Hell Week, in which Steve starred. Once again he was everywhere, no let up. Relentless.

This time his decisions had got him on national TV being pushed to breaking point by specials force operatives from all over the globe. You want the truth? I would have quit within minutes. Yes, minutes.

You have to be made of a special something to continue to keep going as he did, in both gruelling physical and mental tests specifically designed to break him.

Why would a very successful businessman put himself through this? Because he pushes to do and be better all the time, in all aspects.

We can't all be exceptional at everything, but we can be the best we can be. Throughout this book lessons are shared that allowed a normal South London boy to become anything but normal. And following the path he illuminates you can make the same decision to be the best you can be.

Over the last few years we've become friends and this old dog has over that time been taught some new tricks.

Brad Burton
www.bradburton.biz

"A MIND
IS LIKE A
PARACHUTE.
IT DOESN'T WORK
IF IT IS NOT OPEN."

FRANK ZAPPA

Introduction

Full disclosure: The style of this book is not very conventional. But, then again, conventional is not what you need to change your life. The content within the following chapters has been constructed from experience backed by research and draws heavily on the insights gained from over a decade of obsessive study, hosting seminars, self-development and coaching.

I'm no guru. It's safe to say that I am still constantly learning and will continue to do so as long as I'm lucky enough to be alive. I'm a full-time student and a part-time teacher – it is with great pleasure that I can share the knowledge I have accumulated on my journey, the lessons I have learned from my successes and the valuable teachings from the mistakes I've been fortunate enough to make. After all, mastery is a journey not a destination - an asymptote, an unreachable ideal for which we strive but can never actually reach. What we really want is *growth*.

So how can I help you achieve growth? Let's get one thing straight. This is not a 'happy-clappy' book. The title should have given that away. This book is not intended to pat you on the back and tell you *everything is okay*. I'm a nice guy, but to be truly nice you must be truly honest, which means, *no bullshit*. Whilst working your way through this book please always keep in mind that the more you put into this, the more you will get out of it. Don't hold back – the saddest thing about bullshit is that we tend to bullshit ourselves more than anyone else.

We live in a world riddled with insanity. By insanity I do not mean proposed ailments contained within the Diagnostic and Statistical Manual of Mental Disorders, or DSM for short. Well I do, but not in the way you may expect. The actual insanity is the fact that we have such a manual of labels for all that we don't understand. Until the 1970s homosexuality was listed as a disorder! The manual is ever expanding with new alleged disorders being added with each update, such as 'internet gaming disorder'.

The scary thing is that in a case where somebody does have a mental or emotional challenge and really needs help, what they often get instead is an unhelpful diagnostic label. The very suggestion you have such a disorder can make you believe it, making it a self-fulfilling prophecy. In some instances a label gives the perfect excuse to not rectify the problem. We often hear people trade their socially accepted excuses.

In many cases instead of changing behaviour people take drugs that simply mask their symptoms, or even worsen them in the long term. According to health service figures Prozac was prescribed in the UK 4.2 million times on the NHS between 2010 and 2011. Prozac comes with a warning from the NHS that users may experience suicidal tendencies whilst on the drug, somewhat of a paradox. It is tantamount to suggesting you take a diet pill that will make you gain weight.

Whatever your stance on psychiatric medications the bottom line is that they fail to deal with the root cause of the issue. It is like chopping a weed down and never treating the root to prevent further growth. It will continue to grow. It is insanity at its finest. The problem here is a method of thinking that is unresourceful. It is this that should and can be dealt with. When we do things properly we can instil real and sustainable change in our lives.

The aim of this book is to do exactly that, pull out the roots and make sure the weeds never come back. There are no side effects here, using this book will not cause birth defects, impotence, constipation or otherwise. The only warning I am obliged to give is that life will never be the same.

Make sure that you keep a notepad and pen to hand **at all times** whilst reading for use during the chapter challenges. During the final burn be sure to write down the darkest, deepest, most disturbing thoughts – no procrastinating – and rest safely knowing that once you carry out the physical act of burning them absolutely *no one* will be able to see them ever again. Yes, there will be burning involved. The bottom line with these beliefs is that if you don't burn them they will end up burning you from the inside out.

Seriously though, **<u>DO THE WORK!</u>** I'm not kidding. This book isn't intended for theoretical entertainment. It has been written to tear out all the bullshit lingering in your mind. Many chapters will end with a few short exercises marked as chapter challenges, and only by working through them will you be able to put the lessons into practice.

- It will be challenging at times

- It will provoke you and threaten your current thinking

- It will be painful to face the facts

- It will help you put knowledge into practice. Knowledge is *not* power, it is merely potential until applied.

- It will serve as a catalyst to achieving the life you deserve

- How much you get out of it depends entirely on you

Only a scarce few live anywhere even close to their full potential without advice and encouragement. I have made it my mission to help as many people as I can to unlock their potential and create the life they deserve. Now it's your turn.

***

Often I finish a long book and realise that I could have taken on board the message from the title alone. What lay within the pages were 101 ways to communicate the same point over and over, however valid the point might be. If you are not new to this area of literature you will be all too familiar with this style of 'padded' book.

Don't panic: this will not be a repetitive text.

That said, there is massive value in coming back to this book and repeating this process again and again. Treat it as a manual, not a quick page-turner. After all, practice makes permanent; even in the absence of constructive practice, the things you do day in day out will dictate whatever results and habits you end up cultivating. Those unfocused, unchecked results and habits can easily detract from the greater good if you're not careful, so it's important to continue your personal development throughout your life in order to achieve the best results.

In over a decade of coaching I have listened to hour upon hour of, well, bullshit. I've had the chance to work with all manner of people from young offenders to superstar musicians, lawyers to professional athletes, schoolchildren to pensioners. In this time I have come to realise that some things are apparent across the spectrum: we all have beliefs and there's nothing wrong with that, we need them to survive.

The main consideration then is the effect of the belief, whatever the belief itself may be. I am not ignorant enough to suggest one belief is better than another; what interests me is the effect your beliefs have on you. A positive belief can change the way you feel about yourself and how you make others feel, the precise validity is not what is paramount. The *results* of the belief define the value.

Whether you study scientific, religious or purely personal development literature and whether you incline to be spiritual or pragmatic, it is clear that the desired outcome and ultimate goal within life tends to be the same for all of us: *happiness*. In a world where all that we truly know are our thoughts and our emotions, what else could we logically strive for?

The difference though is the vehicle by which we attempt to travel to that state of happiness. What this is tends to be selected as a result of both individual preference and geographical accident.

Our particular religious belief system, for example, is often chosen for us by inherited culture. If you were born in one part of the world you are more likely to be Muslim than Christian, or more likely to be Sikh than Hindu. In secular parts of the western world if your parents were atheists you may believe that science is our only window on the truth and that nothing exists beyond our physical universe. These are all belief systems, even a belief in nothing constitutes a view of the world.

The particular belief you hold is not an issue. What is important is the extent to which you can adjust your beliefs if they don't serve you in your quest for happiness, contribution and personal fulfilment. One of the many beauties of the world is that you can entertain systems of thinking and acting that serve you, and discard at will those which do nothing for you. As I will discuss later, *flexibility* is a huge strength.

Few would disagree that they would sooner live a life of happiness over a life of sadness; the question we then ask is how we go about acquiring a happy life? We are conditioned at a very young age to believe many inaccurate things and are not equipped as children to challenge the underlying validity of what we are taught. For example, it's engrained within many of us that the quality of our happiness lies in the external world, or that it directly correlates with the quality of our material things – cars, houses, jewellery and clothing.

There is no doubt these things can give pleasure and satisfaction for a while but how many wealthy people are miserable and unfulfilled? Trick question - just as many are not wealthy, no more, no less because finances are not a strong enough variable in the equation of true success. Sadness and suicide afflict rich and poor alike, the true key to happiness is in our emotions, not our wallets. Take Adolf Merkle who committed suicide despite having a net worth of over £8 billion. You could easily label a high net worth individual as successful but committing suicide is the ultimate failure. It is our mindset and the value that we deliver to others that indicate our true success.

Of course there are times when money may induce a state of happiness (more often than not only temporarily), but couldn't it also be proposed that this comes about as the result of the many years of social conditioning to which we are all subjected that makes us see wealth as the solution to all our problems? Surely if emotion is an internal mental state, then the answer to how to live a happy life must also lie within.

When asked what they want, people will often present me with a cascade of goals based entirely in the external world. This is absolutely fine. However, it's usually a good guarantee that there's an emotion buried beneath whatever it is they're aspiring to, regardless of their stated goals.

For example: you may want to own a certain car, to volunteer in an orphanage, to run a marathon, or to land on the moon (I still haven't let go of this one). The reason for each specific goal, once you trace them back far enough, is that completing them will make you feel good. You'll be happy. Whilst it's fantastic to do this, it's always worth bearing in mind that happiness comes from within and can be experienced at any time: it's a choice, not an outcome. Don't put off your right to experience happiness and don't forget to enjoy the journey towards completing your goals.

Regardless of what's happening in your life right this second, there's always at least one thing you can focus on that will give you a reason to be happy. In order to make this point I am going to make a basic assumption and guess that if you are reading this, you are currently alive. You are a living and breathing human being. You are therefore already a *winner*.

Disagree? Single-handedly you defeated around 250 million others in a race to exist. You were stronger than the rest. The odds of winning the UK lottery are 1 in 14 million. You're 1 in 250 million. You're a born winner. The odds get incomprehensibly slimmer when you go back in time, tracing your lineage and all the impossible probabilities for all *their* paths crossing before you and them in turn winning their race. That adds some perspective to your life, doesn't it? What other seemingly unlikely possibilities are just lying before you waiting for you to open your mind to them?

CHAPTER CHALLENGE

ACCOUNTABILITY

Take **5 minutes** and consider all of the possible reasons you may fail to complete the challenges in this book. You **MUST** write these answers down for this exercise to work. Be honest. The more honest you are now, the easier we can prevent that failure happening! *(Don't move on until you have completed this first section, complete the exercise in order and make sure you actually **write** the answers down)*

Example: I failed this book because... I was scared.

1. I failed this book because...

2. I failed this book because...

3. I failed this book because...

4. I failed this book because...

5. I failed this book because...

Now let's do the opposite. List all the reasons why you will be successful at completing this book. Take **5 minutes** and consider all of the possible reasons you will have to complete the challenges in this book. Say what you believe you will achieve, why it is important to you, how you will do it. Don't overthink it, just let the answers flow and write them down as they come to you.

Example: I was successful with this book because... I allocated time for self-improvement.

1. I was successful with this book because...

2. I was successful with this book because...

3. I was successful with this book because...

4. I was successful with this book because...

5. I was successful with this book because...

Firstly, a quick thank you for not jumping ahead! For this part you won't need to write anything. Take your answers to Part 1 and Part 2 and replace the word **book** with **life**. Then read back all of the answers to yourself...

Wait for it...

Congratulations, you've just successfully defeated your very first bit of bullshit! Easy, wasn't it? There's a lot more where that came from...

FOR THERE IS NOTHING
EITHER GOOD OR BAD,
BUT THINKING MAKES IT SO

HAMLET (2.2:11)

CHAPTER 1

You'd better believe it

There are two types of beliefs: **empowering** and **disempowering**. You may already know them as positive and negative (or limiting).

One thing they are absolutely and categorically *not* is right and wrong. We would be a step beyond ignorant to ever value-judge the beliefs of others. With such an eclectic mixture of opinions on offer, inspired by different life experiences and learnings, nobody on this planet has the right to judge the beliefs of another and doing so leads more often than not to conflict. We will look simply at whether or not a belief is of service to you. By that I mean, is it giving or leading you to what you desire from life, whilst allowing others the right to have the same?

Beliefs are what instigate behaviour; both the belief of what something means and subsequently the belief on how to respond to that meaning. Behaviour is the master of results; what we do in this life governs what we get from this world. What happens with us internally can only be ascertained by how we act externally therefore behaviour is all that is measurable in the outside world. Behaviour stems from beliefs. Thus beliefs are the root of our results and can only be quantified by the value of or damage caused by the results that they inspire.

Beliefs are what drove a man to stand up in protest before a convoy of tanks in Tiananmen Square in China and what drove another to fly an American Airlines flight into the World Trade Center in an attack responsible for stealing the lives of thousands. Beliefs can raise people to greatness or destroy entire nations. Your beliefs about your self-worth dictate what you will and won't tolerate from the world. When a group of black teenagers demanded their right to the same education as the white people in their town Little Rock, Arkansas, despite death threats and massive opposition they created a revolution. Our beliefs shape our world. **How are your beliefs shaping your world?**

All of your beliefs have positive intentions. Even the bullshit ones (sometimes they just need some burning to get them in order). Often without conscious consideration, the bullshit belief is achieving the exact *opposite* result to its intention. For example, when our beliefs about a given situation or individual cause us to fear being hurt. We often find that in the process we are hurt by our worry alone, even in the absence of the feared outcome ever materialising.

Studies show that 85% of the things that we worry about never actually happen and of the 15% that do, only a small fraction are avoidable. Of the unavoidable, most are not actually as bad as initially expected. So, although these beliefs are attempting to protect us from suffering they are inadvertently doing just that and causing us to suffer unnecessarily. It is more important to concern ourselves with what lies within our control. Therein lies the question of responsibility.

Responsibility – the ability to respond

The clue is in the name

Beliefs on responsibility have a dramatic impact on the outcome of a situation. For example, on 13th March 1964, 38 people witnessed first-hand the murder of 28-year-old Kitty Genovese. Not a single one of the witnesses made an attempt to help her, or even contact the police whilst the attack was taking place. In contrast, Tilly Smith, who was only 10 years old at the time, cleared an entire beach in Thailand by persistently asserting her suspicion that a Tsunami was imminent after the 2004 Indian Ocean Earthquake had struck.

Following a geography lesson covering the warning signs of Tsunamis two weeks prior, Tilly took responsibility and saved the lives of nearly a hundred people from a tragedy that took hundreds of thousands in total. Thanks to Tilly, Maikhao Beach was one of the few beaches in Thailand with no reported casualties. What would have happened if Tilly had not believed in her ability to respond to the perceived threat?

Sadly, many adults would lack the gumption to exercise this level of bravery. Keeping our heads below the parapet is all too familiar in modern day living. We are rewarded for 'just getting on with it' and not complaining. People are too scared to stand up to their employers for their working rights or to leave a toxic spouse.

The interesting thing about belief is that when we start to believe in ourselves then others begin to believe in us too. When appearing as an investor on the television show 'The Money Pit' I couldn't help but notice that it was those touting for investment with a confident pitch and strong presence that tended to secure investment over those with just a logical business proposition. Many investors in fact state that they buy into people and their passion rather than their product and projections.

Now that you know the power of beliefs you can begin to understand that it is dangerous to harbour bullshit ones and beneficial to house empowering ones. In the next chapter we will look at where many of our beliefs actually come from.

CHAPTER 2

The seeds of all bullshit

We gather beliefs over the years. They change constantly – sometimes gradually, sometimes drastically. When something happens that we really didn't expect or was completely out of our normal area of expectation, we tend to either update our beliefs accordingly or find a contrived justification that aligns with our old belief.

Unfortunately, our beliefs aren't updating regularly enough. There is something called *confirmation bias:* once we have a belief we aim to find evidence to support it. We attempt to confirm our preconceptions and this often leads to mistaken judgements. It's just easier that way and we naturally gravitate towards the easy way of thinking, as is illustrated on the following page in the concept of *cognitive fluency*.

PSYCHOLOGISTS HAVE DETERMINED THAT WE ARE MORE LIKELY TO MOVE TOWARDS THOUGHTS THAT ARE EASIER TO PROCESS. THIS HAS BEEN DEMONSTRATED THROUGH VARIOUS STUDIES, INCLUDING ONE THAT INDICATES A CORRELATION BETWEEN THE EASE OF PRONOUNCING A COMPANY NAME AND THE LIKELIHOOD OF AN INVESTOR BUYING SHARES. WHAT IS MORE INTERESTING IS THAT WE ARE MORE LIKELY TO BELIEVE SOMETHING THAT IS CLEARER, OR EASIER TO UNDERSTAND. A STUDY CARRIED OUT SHOWED THAT CHANGING THE FONT OF TEXT INFLUENCES THE OPINION OF THE READER OF ITS VALIDITY. THE CRUX HERE IS IF YOU WANT TO COMMUNICATE A POINT THEN DO SO WITHOUT HURTING THE OTHER PERSON'S BRAIN AND YOU HAVE A FIGHTING CHANCE. THE ACRONYM K.I.S.S SPRINGS TO MIND; KEEP IT SIMPLE, STUPID.

COGNITIVE FLUENCY

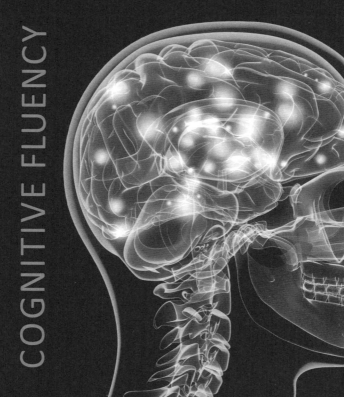

An example of confirmation bias: you meet someone you've heard a lot about (a lot of *bad* stuff) from those whose judgements you value. You now step into the introduction riddled with the negative opinions of others, however subjective. You begin to look for evidence to support your newly adopted beliefs. You scrutinise the details of the interaction and even cast negative meanings on anything ambiguous enough to allow you to do so.

Conversely, if you were interviewing someone for a job whom you believe to be highly intelligent, you may only focus on and notice information that supports that belief. You'd be much more likely to overlook elements inconsistent with your beliefs and maybe even start attributing unlikely meanings onto any inconsistencies that would serve to confirm your preconceptions.

As a psychologist and linguistics tutor I often find that people are analysing my communication in an attempt to uncover the tactics I am using to secretly influence them. Most of the time I am just talking with no agenda, I don't coach unless expressly invited to do so. The fact is, as Freud said when quizzed by his students on the significance of his cigar smoking, 'Sometimes a cigar is just a cigar.'

Author of *The Believing Brain*, Michael Shermer discusses what he has coined as 'belief-dependant realism': once we have instilled a belief we preserve it through an array of cognitive biases that alter our perceptions to fit our beliefs. Amongst the methods of preservation are:

Anchoring Bias: *Relying too heavily on just one piece of information when making decisions*

Authority Bias: *Placing more value in the opinions of a considered authority on a particular matter*

Belief Bias: *Evaluating the integrity of a debate based on the believability of its conclusion*

Confirmation Bias: *Looking for evidence to support existing beliefs and discarding any contrary evidence*

In-group Bias: *Deferring to the beliefs of those who we regard as fellow members*

The challenge is that people don't live in a shared reality, no one does. Nope, not even *you*. We all live in a reality constructed from our personal beliefs. We live entirely at the mercy of the meanings we place upon things. I'll come back to that but don't worry, it doesn't have to be a bad thing.

We develop our beliefs over the years based on our family environment, social interactions, emotional experience, media exposure, and as we will discuss shortly, the education system. We then continue to interact with these beliefs, the good and the bad. Most experts will agree that by late childhood a person's belief system is reasonably well-formed, and their core beliefs are unlikely to alter much throughout the rest of their life without large disruption.

Children are naively egocentric and therefore attribute most circumstances that occur in some way to themselves. If a five year old child's parents argued, the child assumes blame. They are a bad person, no one can love them and they deserve the worst. Left unchecked, the potential damage this misinterpreted experiential learning could cause is obvious.

Stop the bus – let's get off and think about that. Subtract five years from your age, take the answer and consider that that's approximately how long you may have been carrying around some of your most pivotal beliefs. You upgrade the software on your phone every month in order that it performs more efficiently and better fulfils your needs. Why would you not upgrade your beliefs – after *decades*?

Because you're scared. Somewhere within you, deep down where that belief lies, is the same young, childlike mind that created it. You are cautious, worried and concerned that the smallest change in belief could disrupt and dislodge the very foundations that your world of thought rests upon.

According to Deepak Chopra in *Quantum Healing* and echoed by many other experts, although we have an estimated 65,000 thoughts a day, a whopping 95% of those are the same thoughts we had the day prior. How many of those 95% are thoughts we could do without, biased thoughts that support beliefs that run contrary to our development towards a positive, strong and well-intentioned person?

Life isn't about repetition; it is about growth, progress and variety of experience. In order for us to grow it's vital that we step beyond comfort zones, this in turn forces the boundaries of our comfort zone to grow too. We must learn to be comfortable being uncomfortable. Only in that mode can we obliterate any bullshit beliefs and reconnect with our true self.

CHAPTER CHALLENGE

CELEBRATE GOOD TIMES

Now it's time for you to do the work! Let's get rid of some more bullshit patterns and step into a new life. Go to a crowded place such as a coffee shop, shopping centre, restaurant, bar or library. Casually stop whatever you are doing and break out into a sudden, unprompted, loud and animated celebration for 5-10 seconds. It is important that you hold it for that long so we can sustain the discomfort for a moment and ensure that people know it is you.

- Do not have your phone on you. No pretending you got a message or otherwise. This is you celebrating for no reason, no cover story permitted

- Celebrations may include: jumping, shouting, whooping and punching the air. Keep it family friendly!

- Be loud! Make sure that you gain people's attention

- Laughing afterwards to yourself is fine, but smiling awkwardly at others is not. You're not doing it for anyone else

- Do this alone, no strength in numbers. No hand-holding and no spectators. This is a solo challenge for a reason

- If you are quizzed on what's going on just explain that you are having a fantastic day and wish them a fantastic day too!

Congratulations for daring to break free from the prison of self-conscious restraint. This challenge will disrupt any inhibiting patterns of self-talk, the same self-talk that stops you from asking for a date with that guy or girl at the gym, or stops you from telling your boss where specifically to stick their job. You will invariably hear the same voices before you perform this celebration; they will question the value, attempt to dissuade you. Simply thank them for their opinion and do it anyway. This is about taking ownership back over your mind. You will finish feeling liberated and ready to do anything.

IN SCHOOL, YOU'RE TAUGHT A LESSON AND THEN GIVEN A TEST. IN LIFE, YOU'RE GIVEN A TEST THAT TEACHES YOU A LESSON

TOM BODETT

CHAPTER 3

What happened?

A great deal of this harmful conditioning comes from our social environment as children. Sadly, there are major flaws in our current education system and the effects are devastating. We are given a great deal of information at school (and I'm a big fan of information), but we aren't taught *application.* That's just the tip of this political rant. You see, there is a distinct difference between *thinking* and *doing*; the ability to *do* comes not just from knowledge but also and more importantly from the belief in one's ability to utilise that knowledge. How do we learn to believe in our ability to *do*?

Knowledge isn't power. Knowledge is merely *potential* power. "Knowledge **applied** is power" – that's closer to the truth. Otherwise it's like writing down the winning lottery numbers and not playing them. You can't spend *potential* winnings in the shops!

How many times have you met someone with all the knowledge but still living a second-rate life? Coaching is a perfect example. I train many coaches, some of whom seem to have more deeply ingrained issues than many of my regular clients. Worse than that; they tend to know the answers but don't apply them! Some are great at coaching others but fail to apply their lessons to themselves. Rule number one to all coaches reading this: get high on your own supply - your first client is yourself.

I don't believe we are taught to actually think for ourselves in school. In fact, I remember on two occasions, once in science and once in maths, being kicked out of class for raising my hand and questioning the content. School was a rollercoaster experience for me. Accepting what was presented to me at face value was not something I was able to do. I realised at a young age that teachers don't *always* know best (perhaps I was a tad too vocal about that at times). Problem-solving is a life skill and aside from linear examples such as maths puzzles, schools don't encourage this kind of cognitive engagement.

Schools are effectively conditioning us for working life. We turn up on time, listen and do as we are told. I would hasten to add here that although I am a businessman and have no intention of ever being an employee again, I am not ignorant enough to attempt to be condescending. Often I meet 'entrepreneurs' that tell me how foolish people who work for someone else are, how everyone should leave their job and go it alone. So I'll ask them, *who do you suppose is going to be working for you and running your business one day then?*

There is a need for diversity and variety in society; we can't all have our own businesses and quite frankly not everyone wants to. Some people are content with a steady income, so long as they have overheads covered and are able to make provisions for their family – what's wrong with that? But, if it's something that you want to do and you aren't afraid to aim high, then you need to burn the bullshit and get a wiggle on.

SCHOOL VERSUS ARNOLD SCHWARZENEGGER

SCHOOL

6 RULES FOR SUCCESS:
1 - WHAT THE TEACHER SAYS GOES
2 - FOLLOW THE RULES
3 - FAILING IS EMBARRASSING AND SHAMEFUL
4 - MY DREAMS ARE UNREALISTIC
5 - COMPLETE ONLY THE WORK GIVEN
6 - EVERY MAN FOR HIMSELF

ARNIE

6 RULES FOR SUCCESS:
1 - TRUST YOURSELF
2 - BREAK SOME RULES
3 - DO NOT BE AFRAID TO FAIL
4 - IGNORE THE NAYSAYERS
5 - WORK LIKE HELL
6 - GIVE BACK

ARNIE IS AN EXTREMELY ACCOMPLISHED MAN AND HE OFFERS FANTASTIC TRANSFERABLE WISDOM. DESPITE ADVERSITY AND THE ODDS, HE LEFT HIS VILLAGE IN AUSTRIA TO PURSUE HIS DREAM TO BECOME A WORLD CHAMPION BODYBUILDER, THEN WENT ON TO BECOME ONE OF THE WORLD'S MOST FAMOUS ACTORS (DESPITE HIS THICK ACCENT), AND LATER THE GOVERNOR OF CALIFORNIA. HIS REPEATED SUCCESSES ARE A TESTAMENT TO THE VALIDITY OF HIS METHODS.

Following from the *blame,* I would like to now *disclaim*. There may well be flaws in the education system and life can be a challenge, but there's no excuse for living in a culture of finger-pointing.

I've set out all the anti-school rhetoric above in order to bring the situation to your awareness. It's *your* responsibility to educate yourself. We may live in a blame culture, but it's *your* life nevertheless; getting mad helps no one, least of all yourself. I do genuinely believe education systems are set up and run with positive intentions and by great people – they just may not always be satisfying the greater good as their resources are lacking.

Education: from the Latin *ēducātiō* , *ēdūcō* ("I lead forth, I take out; I raise up, I erect") from *ē-* ("from, out of") and *dūcō* ("I lead, I conduct")

To *educate* means to draw something from within – this suggests that it was already there *a priori*.

By definition, education is not the transplantation of knowledge and wisdom; it's the *bringing out* or facilitation of learning, and it would serve us well to remember that the responsibility to learn rests on our shoulders. Whether we know it or not, it always has done.

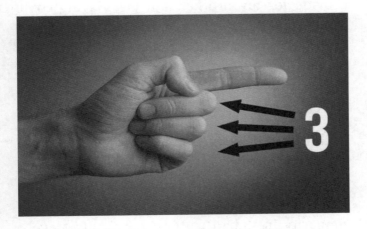

Remember that whenever you point your finger there are three more pointing back at you.

If you want something done...

School didn't prepare me to be an entrepreneur. My Dad did. Entrepreneurship was a by-product of my upbringing. I come from a working class family; my parents worked extremely hard and often around the clock to provide for my brother and me. Having come from scarcity and a family that had struggled at times to buy food, my father valued security highly and placed no great value in life's luxuries, such as designer clothes or fancy vehicles.

He drove the same car for 17 years before admitting defeat and has owned the same kitchen for decades because 'there's nothing wrong with it.' Incidentally, I noticed a beautiful similarity in Cuban culture during my travels, not having the option of living in the throwaway culture that we do. Instead, they have shops along the streets where people would take their old items to be fixed.

As a youngster, I was shuttled around to swimming lessons, judo classes, chess clubs and any other developmental practices that I would enthusiastically agree to but when I would ask for a games console, my dad said no, 'it's a waste of money.' Invariably he was right, but the pressure was on me socially as a young person to have a console. I had to think fast, and in order to get what I wanted *I would have to do it myself.*

Now that's what I call a golden nugget

Little did I realise it at the time, but this was a blessing beyond any other. Into the fridge I went and knocked up some of my favourite salad wraps and chucked them in my bag. I would then go on to sell them at school to generate income (until my Mum cottoned on and put an end to my supply chain). 100% mark-up was good whilst it lasted but I quickly had to reassess and start again; reinvigorated, I started up my copied CD business, selling the latest albums until I had gained enough funds to buy my first PlayStation.

Armed with my new skills in the art of forging and replication, I would borrow games from friends (and sometimes the video store) and make a copy for myself. The only other problem was that within a short time after I had managed to buy my PlayStation, it's newer, flashier replacement came out.

I'm not telling you this in the hope you will start selling sandwich wraps and copied CDs. The point I'm making here is that in life, it pays to learn to think for yourself. I would say *think outside of the box* – but that very box is the one I'm challenging you to disassemble through the lessons within these few pages.

When we ask our parents for a console and they buy it for us, we learn nothing. They buy this out of love, the intentions are positive but we are left with an untrue representation of how the world works. We grow up believing that we get what we want without earning it. This presents many issues later in life.

The truth? If you want to *have* something, you have to *do* something. The answer might not always be obvious, but there is always an answer.

SHARED BELIEF CREATES
THE ILLUSION OF TRUTH

CHAPTER 4

Bullshit goes in,
bullshit comes out

How do we know what we know? How can we be sure what we know? The study of knowledge and justified belief is known as *epistemology*: the consideration of how true something is that we assume we know.

To begin with, let's take a look at how we receive information. We have five *obvious* senses: visual (sight), auditory (hearing), kinaesthetic (touch), olfactory (smell) and gustatory (taste). Through these five senses we constantly process the world around us.

Now what do I mean by bullshit *goes in*? Let's use sight as an example. We are aware there is a colour spectrum, and we also know that we cannot see the entire spectrum – for example, infrared and ultraviolet are out of our range.

Based on this we can agree that our sense of sight is limited. The same thing goes for our auditory sense – we can't hear a dog whistle, for example. Two straightforward instances where we're limited in what we experience in the world around us.

It stands to reason then that our experience of what is real is already a diluted version of what is really there. In addition to this, considering the size of the universe, there must be a myriad of phenomena occurring that our five senses alone can't detect.

To take it one step further, studies now show that there are no predetermined perceptions ascribed to each wavelength of light. This means that when we first make sense of the world we assign our own colour interpretations to different wavelengths. What I see as blue may be what you see as red and vice versa. Scientists say that the huge difference in a perceived colour does *not* affect our experience of the colour. I find this interesting because it supports the fact that what we react to are the meanings we assign to different things. We can both sit and enjoy a beautiful sunset regardless of the literal visual representation because the associations we have formed with those colours make our interpretation of the event beautiful.

Nothing pleases me more than a tasty grey apple

But wait – there's more. Even with the mere five senses that we have, we can only cognitively process a limited amount of information at any one time. According to George Miller, we can only entertain seven plus or minus two bits of information in our 'working memory'. Now let's consider how many bits of information are coming at us in any given second - it's literally millions. We are obviously missing a fair bit. So how do we decide what to pay attention to and what to discard?

We use our experience to unconsciously filter what we consider to be important. If I tell you to pay attention to the feeling and sensations in your left foot at this moment you will be able to detect the feeling of your shoe, sock or the floor against your foot, depending on how you are currently attired and positioned. Now this information was always there but was being filtered as unimportant or irrelevant. The same applies to the way we filter information to support our beliefs about the world and discard things that don't align.

What we focus on becomes our reality. Our world is our thoughts, nothing more. The good news is you can choose what to focus on. That's the beauty of being human.

Maurice DeCastro (author of *Hamster to Harmony*) once explained this to me: "Stephen, the dog knows he is in the room; but he *doesn't* know that he knows he is in the room." Although the dog is thinking, he is not thinking about his thinking – and so is unable to change it.

Thinking about our thinking is what gives us the edge. When we realise we can select our thoughts and not live at the mercy of our environment, we take charge of our lives. This is called going *meta* (beyond).

Let's try a quick demonstration to emphasise the importance of focus:

- Firstly, I would like you to take twenty seconds to scan the room you are currently in. Whilst doing so take note of everything that you can see that is **red**. Take a mental note of how many things and where they are. **Do this before reading on.**

- Now, I would like you to close your eyes for twenty seconds as soon as you finish reading this sentence and list off everything that you saw that was **blue**. Go!

- Now have a quick look round and notice everything you can that is **blue**. Note anything obvious that you missed.

How did you get on? I'm going to assume the same as I did when I was first introduced to this. When you're looking around for everything **red**, you are filtering everything that is **blue**. This is how our focus directs us every day. If we are having a bad day and feeling disenchanted about the world, we look around and find as many things as we can to support our belief that all is non-ideal. We miss all of the great stuff happening because we are filtering it out. Many would go as far as to say this negativity will also undoubtedly *attract* even more bad things into your life.

The answer then: focus on the good. See the opportunity and not the obstacle. Delete the rubbish and amplify the desirable. *What you appreciate, appreciates.* Set yourself a series of questions that precondition your mind to find the silver lining to every cloud.

RAS

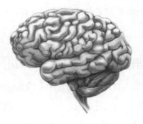

We have something the size of a pinkie finger in our brain called the reticular activating system (RAS) that directs our focus and attention. It is like the gatekeeper to our consciousness, deciding what shall pass. When you make a decision to buy an obscure colour car in a bid to be different, it is the RAS that will kindly draw your attention to the many others that exist on the day you drive off the garage forecourt.

The great news is that the more that we consciously direct our focus and attention the more we can influence that gatekeeper, altering the prioritisation and subsequent processing of incoming information.

CHAPTER CHALLENGE

GET TUNED IN

Every morning I ask myself a series of questions to stimulate and tune in my RAS. What am I excited about today? What do I want to finish this day thinking? What am I grateful for? What makes me feel happiness and why? Who makes me feel happiness and why?

Searching for answers to these questions tunes me in to a wealth of possibilities and opportunities that I may have otherwise missed and have made a profound difference to my quality of life.

I would like to invite you now to create your own series of questions that you will ask yourself every morning. I like to write the answers down as that way I can read them back at a later date which I find enjoyable, but you are free to just answer them in your mind if you prefer.

Create 5 questions that are personal to you, that you believe will stimulate and direct your focus where it needs to go. Think about what you want to achieve and who you want to be and write the questions that first spring to mind.

Next, ask yourself these questions as soon as you wake up in the morning. Give 3 answers to each individual question. This will only take you about five minutes (less than 1% of your day) and will influence the quality of your thoughts for the day – which will alter the course of your life. Easily worth the investment.

REALITY IS WRONG.
DREAMS ARE FOR REAL

-TUPAC SHAKUR

CHAPTER 5

What do you think of that?

The lies we tell other people are nothing compared to the lies we tell ourselves – **Derek Landy**

So now we have received our raw data, what next? Does it just sit there in our minds identical to how it sits in the 'real' world? Of course not! We add our own meanings to what we interpret based on a number of things: our current emotional state, beliefs about the world, past experiences, and whatever else might be influencing us right at that moment. We are constantly altering and omitting information. We can easily miss things that are directly in front of us (as we saw with the focus exercise above), but we can also change them to line up with our experience of the world.

Here's an embarrassing example of how I formed some misinformation based on a temporary emotional state. At the age of 7, my parents took me away on holiday with them, where I fell asleep whilst they popped out to the shops. Just in case I woke up my mum left me a note: *'Don't leave the room, stay in bed. We will be back soon'.*

When I woke up in this strange hotel room and realised my parents weren't there, I began to panic. My young and wild imagination was flooded with disturbing thoughts that my parents had abandoned me or that something terrible had happened to them!

Then I found the note. Great news, this'll explain everything, right? Think again. Given my emotional state (*state* being the perfect word at this point to describe my shaken 7 year old self), I snatched up the note and completely misread the information on the paper, the garbled words somehow reforming themselves through my tears: *'Don't leave any room in the bed. We won't be back'.* Of course they didn't actually write that they wouldn't be back, but I was so ready to believe that reality that I distorted the information – although I was only 7 there, this is the kind of thing we continue to do all throughout life.

Now for a slightly more up-to-date example. Whilst in training school for the London Fire Brigade, there was a typical slacker of a trainee I knew in my squad who was relentlessly late. In an emergency service (let alone in life) this is at very least *somewhat* unacceptable.

One day a senior officer joined us in the afternoon. Whilst stood on parade the two of them locked eyes. Knowing his previous track record, he boomed, "Were you on time this morning?" Blue moon – for the first time I could ever remember, the trainee actually *had* been on time this particular day.

"*Yes*, sir."

"WHY *NOT*?"

This got its fair share of laughs, not the least from the officer himself. He'd distorted what was otherwise clear information in order to support his beliefs (in this instance about an individual who you will be relieved to hear won't be called on to extinguish much anytime soon).

These are great examples of misinterpreting straightforward exchanges. Imagine what happens when some ambiguity is thrown in the mix! What's important is that we maintain sensory acuity; we pay attention to the actual information being presented to us. We do our best *not* to distort it. We see it for what it is and leave our prejudices to one side.

You must be shapeless, formless, like water. When you pour water in a cup, it becomes the cup. When you pour water in a bottle, it becomes the bottle. When you pour water in a teapot, it becomes the teapot. Water can drip and it can crash. Become like water, my friend.

Bruce Lee

CHAPTER 6

Creature vs Creator

People tend to fall in one of two distinct categories:

<u>CREATURES</u> OF CIRCUMSTANCE,

OR

<u>CREATORS</u> OF CIRCUMSTANCE

You either *make* things happen, or you claim they happen *to* you.

This subtle difference in thinking can be the difference between happiness and sadness, being a champion and not even starting the race.

***

I am *allergic* to excuses. You should be too. Day in day out, people recite their socially acceptable reasons for their shortfalls rather than accept culpability. *Yes*, in the short term this may serve to alleviate the pain of the truth, but in the long term this will follow you around like a black storm cloud in a Tom and Jerry cartoon.

The problem is that if you don't accept the degree of influence you have over the events that occur in your life, then you can't take steps to rectify and improve them. A creature will explain to you how the government has stitched them up, or their employer let them down. *It's always someone else's fault for them*.

A creator, however, will say, 'since someone else has changed *this*, I'll change *that*.' They lose no sleep over it and keep the ball rolling, focusing on what is in their control. They diversify; they see the opportunity and *not* the obstacle.

The ability to diversify comes through *flexibility*. Flexibility is critical. Flexibility can be improving a way of approaching a situation or changing it all together.

The measure of intelligence is the ability to change – Albert Einstein

Being flexible means being open to more potential options. Flexibility doesn't spell weakness or passivity. On the contrary – it's a powerful tool. To lack flexibility usually signifies ignorance. Going about the same thing, with the same approach, despite no progress – doesn't that sound like madness to you? When you aren't getting the results that you want, you have to change your approach and try again. If it doesn't work the first time, change your approach again and again and again and again. Keep trying until you reach your desired outcome. You'll get there.

A puncher's chance

It's the 70s. A man earning $36 a week as an usher writes a script for a movie and takes it to a production company. They reject the script. He has a choice now, accept the rejection or try somewhere else. He tries somewhere else. They reject it too. Again and again, with varied approaches, he tries until he is rejected 50 times in total.

Again, he approaches another company. Boom! They love it; they put up big money to buy the rights to it.

'No. I want to star in it'.

They refuse. He persists.

He stands his ground until *they* come to an agreement. After lengthy battles between the producers and the film company, slashing budgets because of the dreamer's tenacity and forcing the producers to re-mortgage their houses to finance the film's release, it went on to win Oscars and become one of the highest grossing films and, arguably, one of the most enjoyable of all time.

The film was *Rocky*, if you haven't yet guessed and the actor Sylvester Stallone. The very theme of persistence and never giving up is prevalent throughout the film itself. Not bad for a man who parked cars for a living. As the fictional character Rocky Balboa says himself in Rocky V: 'If you know what you're worth, then go out and get what you're worth!'

Against the odds

Creators believe in themselves. They listen and take on board what others say, but ultimately they believe in themselves. There are countless examples of hugely successful people who defied the odds to create their desired destiny.

- Albert Einstein was thought to be mentally backward prior to changing the face of science. He has since been regarded as one of the most intelligent humans to have graced this planet.

- Walt Disney was sacked for lacking imagination by his local newspaper and then went bankrupt. He is now a cultural icon and the epitome of creativity.

- Colonel Sanders received over a thousand rejections before someone agreed to stock his fried chicken (known better as KFC). Now you can't turn a corner without seeing one of his stores.

- After being told by teachers that he was too stupid to learn anything Thomas

Edison invented the lightbulb after over 1000 attempts, altering the course of history.

- Michael Jordan was cut from his high school basketball team for not being good enough. He is now listed on the NBA website as 'the greatest basketball player of all time.'

- JK Rowling was broke and depressed before she wrote Harry Potter. She has now sold over 400 million copies of her books and is a billionaire as result.

CHAPTER CHALLENGE

CREATE A CIRCUMSTANCE

Right now think of 3 seemingly absurd things that you want to achieve (given a world of infinite possibilities). Put pen to paper. You know the rules. Whether there is a cause that you want to be a part of in a third world country or a house that you dream of owning, a car you want to drive or marathon that you would like to run. Choose that absurd or outrageous goal and take one small step towards making it a reality.

I did a very similar exercise once and as part of the action phase I went online and found the house of my dreams, with a swimming pool, gym and the big automatic gates I had always craved. In hindsight, with six bathrooms, it was maybe a bit over the top but that is ultimately the exact point of this. Only when you are ready to go a bit too far will you realise how far you are able to go.

Next, take one step towards achieving them. Towards making them become a reality.

Imagine what you would do if they were a real possibility. For me this meant phoning the agent and booking a viewing for the home. Pretending that I could actually afford it. *Acting as if.*

For you this could be phoning the company of your dreams to ask for information on working there. Enquiring about charity work abroad. Booking a test drive for a Lamborghini. Don't sell yourself short. Make sure it involves speaking to real people face to face, not just firing off an email. Know what it means to become the people that do these things by pretending to be them.

In case you are wondering, I actually moved into the house after meeting the agent, and what had appeared completely impossible became possible when I actually gave it some careful consideration. You have 24 hours to get moving with this. **No excuses!**

The Jam Pizza

A long time before I began delivering dreams, I delivered pizzas. As the phones buzzed with Friday night's usual flurry of orders I grabbed one and took the call in an effort to alleviate the strain on my colleagues.

"How can I help you?" I beamed down the phone, happy to be of service.

"Oh hello there," said a calm elderly voice cutting through the chaos surrounding me within the busy store.

"How can I help?" I repeated politely in an attempt to elicit an order.

"I would like to try one of these pizza things."

"Great, what kind of pizza would you like?" I said enthusiastically. The phone went silent.

After a few moments she resurfaced, "Oh, I don't know – I didn't know there were different types." I pointed out that there were many varieties of pizza, the main difference was the topping. What topping would she like?

"Just jam or something, I suppose."

At that, my heart joined the mozzarella in the oven and melted. I elegantly persuaded her to scrap the jam idea and go for something a bit tastier. She agreed.

Not many things stick quite so clearly in my head from my days as a pizza delivery driver; this seemingly trivial phone call touched my heart in a strange way. Pondering on it I realised I had learned something.

Firstly, it is never too late to try new things. The admiration I had for the bravery of this lady was overwhelming. I made sure to personally take the order out to her. Secondly, there is strength in vulnerability. It isn't always necessary to know all there is to know before you take action.

You are always inspiring others. Little did the elderly lady know how much merely ordering her pizza meant to me, and what an impact it would have on my future. Someone is always taking heed of our actions: make sure those actions demonstrate the message and example that you want them to.

CHAPTER 7

If you can see it, you can be it!

Simple really, isn't it? See it, be it.

If you can recognise a quality that you wish to adopt, you're more than capable of using it. Note I say *use* it, not learn it; you already have that quality within you. The fact that you can recognise something means you have the capacity to understand it and represent it.

Let's contextualise for a minute and think about the concept of *confidence.* It's undeniably an important trait to have at your disposal. In order to interpret confident behaviour from an individual you must be able to pick out the characteristics that a confident person would display. For example, you may recognise someone is confident from what they say. You certainly have the ability to repeat words. You may recognise it from the way they stand; you can certainly adopt your posture to mirror this. You may see confident breathing, tonality and so forth, which are all easily imitable too.

If you can see it, you can be it. The trick is to then model what you see, to take on the characteristics and act as if.

Does this make you confident or are you just being a good actor? The only way really of gauging someone's confidence is through behaviour. There is no other way of measuring someone's *internal* state than the calibration and subsequent interpretation of their external state. Behaviour is then the only effective measure of someone's internal composition, and ultimately it makes no difference if you initially feel as if you're merely acting a confident role – if you're showing this externally then you will get the same results. Needless to say it'll also be mirrored internally too.

Here, however, it might be wise to speak of the difference between *calibration* (a measurement of a factual occurrence) and *interpretation* (the meaning you believe a factual occurrence bore). It is dangerous and counterproductive to confuse the two.

A textbook example is the crossing of your arms, as anyone who has been on even the most second-rate body language course may nod at in agreement. Some courses will explain to you that folded arms are negative or closed body language. My question to you would be have you ever folded your arms when you have been neither closed nor negative? Of course you have! Perhaps you were cold. The upshot then is that this *interpretation* that someone is negative or closed is rubbish, there are obviously other things at play that might lead to your crossing your arms.

The skill is to practice noticing without placing a meaning or *interpretation* on a particular behaviour. The consequences of getting this wrong are dire. When someone asks you if you have a problem (and you are perfectly fine), what tends to happen? You *now* have a problem - you don't feel that person understands you. And everyone wants to be understood.

Another example of this gone wrong is through the teaching of eye accessing patterns. Years ago it was discovered that in order to access certain areas of our brain we move our eyes in certain directions. The upper plane tends to be visual, the middle plane corresponds to our auditory faculties, while moving our eyes in the lower plane of vision is related to emotions or linked to our inner dialogue.

As a rule of thumb for a right-handed person, their eyes will tend to look up and to their left for a visual recollection and, conversely, up and to the right for a visual construct. If I asked perhaps the colour of your previous car you tend to find eyes will go up and to the left. If I ask you to visualise how it would have looked in pink they will then likely head up and right to construct that image. Don't believe me? Try it on someone who doesn't know you are doing it. The trick is to ask a question that isn't sitting on top of their mind so they have to actually dig a bit for the answer.

This model is often misrepresented and misused. The patterns are referred to as ways of detecting lies. It can prove a lucrative prospect for some as it plays into an insecure desire to question the validity of surface level communication. People are often told that if someone looks up and to the right then they are making something up. Bull. We can never expect to understand the actual thoughts of an individual by their eye patterns alone. It is merely a single demonstration of how they process information.

Every single person should be taken at face value as we are all beautifully diverse. As they say, to assume makes an **ass** of **u** and **me**. I have heard of people returning from a course teaching eye patterns and ditching their spouse of ten years on the strength of a demonstration of eye patterning. Dismissing years of understanding someone for a technique that they hardly even comprehend!

So, you can see the personality trait and you know you can develop it yourself, what's next? Next, we *model*. Modelling is breaking down a behaviour and then copying it. This happens on many levels – not just physiologically but also at a belief level. What beliefs does this person hold? What language do they use when communicating with others? From this we can also deduce what language they will use when communicating with themselves. Once you have fully understood the underlying aspects of the trait in their totality, you can then begin to replicate and model these.

Success is non-discriminatory. It doesn't care who you are rather what you do.

CHAPTER CHALLENGE

READY TO MODEL?

- Take someone you admire or take inspiration from. This can be a famous person, a family member or anyone you choose. Heck even a superhero.

- Identify five characteristics that you admire about that person.

- Write a few lines on how you believe they got them and how you can replicate their successes.

The more accurately you can understand and replicate the behaviour of another, the more easily you reproduce their results.

CHAPTER 8

Body language of a champion

We know that one's internal state is often clearly demonstrated through overt physiology. The slumped shoulders, drooping head and frowning face – we all know how to detect these and other classic emotional cues from very early on. Our tone also tends to run in alignment with our mood; we know when someone is sulking or ecstatic from the way they say what they say. Yet physiology and one's mental state are not too dissimilar to the chicken and egg paradox. Your body language and tonality don't merely reflect your internal emotions – they are in fact often the cause. This is great news as it means we can consciously utilise them to influence our emotions.

When we open our body language and adopt more empowering expressions, we communicate to our mind to also open up. Another added bonus is the way this non-verbal communication is received by others. We have all heard the old saying, extracted (and often misrepresented) from the work of Albert Mehrabian in 1971 that only 7% of our communication is words. The remainder is comprised of 55% body language and 38% tonality. Whether you agree with the precise statistics or not, it's clear that a huge chunk of our communication lies beyond our words alone.

People often say they can hear a smile through the phone – *this* is tonality. As Mehrabian elucidated, if there happens to be any incongruence between your words and your tonality, 86% of the time people will trust what they gauge from tonality alone over what was communicated to them in the content of the words themselves. This is also true of our inner dialogue. Often referred to as *sub-modalities*; the difference in tone, speed, volume, pace, analogue marking and so forth as we form it internally is bound to influence the reception externally.

Try it for yourself! First, try saying *just like that!* In a voice of judgement and anger. See how it makes you feel to attack yourself in that tone. If you close your eyes and really allow yourself to experience the tonality, what physiological and emotional response do you realise?

Now, try the same phrase again – *Just like that* - but proudly, as though you were bragging at how well you completed a task. How does this make you feel? What do you notice? I'm sure the two responses are totally different. Response influences behaviour, which in turn determines results.

Repeat the same phrase in your mind one last time; but this time whisper it in an attractive and seductive tone. *Just like that.* Need I say more?

***

When it comes to our body language and facial expression, there has been extensive research done around the link between psychology and physiology. For example, certain body postures stimulate specific areas of the brain, creating feelings of happiness. Armed with this knowledge we can consciously utilise our body posture to instil regular happiness in ourselves.

Smiling is something that has been widely studied. Amongst the better-known studies is the 1989 work by Robert Zajonc in which subjects participated in a blind experiment to repeat vowel sounds such as a long 'e' or long 'u', stretching the edges of the mouth or forcing the mouth upwards into a pout. Subjects reported feeling good after an 'e' and feeling bad after a 'u' sound.

Similar studies have been performed with equivalent results. One asked participants to hold a pen in their mouth either by pouting and holding the pen with their lips or holding it horizontally between their teeth, forcing their mouth into a smile-like position. They all conclude that there is a clear cause and effect relationship between the physical performance of a smile and the psychological response. There is varied speculation as to why this is but it's not too important to us *why* something is how it is.

Rather, now that we know *what* it is we can consider *how* we can use it to our advantage. You don't need to study the root in order to pick the fruit.

A final point on body language: the poses we adopt when confident involve making our bodies bigger whilst being nervous tends to do the opposite. A study conducted by Amy Cuddy, Caroline Wilmouth and Dana Carney from Harvard Business School shows the benefits of adopting 'power poses' prior to 'high-stakes social evaluation' (elsewhere explored in Amy Cuddy's fantastic TED talk, *Your body language shapes who you are*). They asked candidates to adopt either high or low power poses for a two-minute period. When high power poses were adopted prior to a controlled job interview, people achieved greater success and were more likely to perform, while the opposite was also true.

We know then that it is important to adopt particular behaviour in order to elicit desirable emotions, which in turn results in more desirable behaviour. Behaviour is the single most important factor governing the results we achieve in the external world. Acting as if we are already confident, happy or otherwise is then bound to influence our ability to become so. In other words, *fake it until you make it true.*

CHAPTER CHALLENGE

CHUMP TO CHAMP

Stand up. I mean it. You are alive, so act like it. You may want to do this in private. Or you may wish to stop caring so much about what people don't actually think about you. For the first part of this challenge adopt the physiology that you would if you were feeling low energy or upset. How would you have to stand? Where would your shoulders be? What would your breathing be like, shallow or deep? See what you notice about your self-talk. What would you need to say to yourself to feel down? Note where your eyes go. Odds are that to truly feel down you will need to adopt a very downward, sloped and defeated physiology.

Now make like Taylor Swift and shake that off. Wiggle your arms around. Shake like a soggy dog and eject all of the negative energy.

Next, stand up tall, breathe deeply into your diaphragm and fully extend your arms up in the air with hands spread open as though you are celebrating. Place a big cheesy grin on your face and look upwards to the ceiling. Whilst in this pose attempt to recreate the negative self-talk that you carried out so well in the previous stance. Keep the smile and try your best to feel as down as you did before.

I could just explain the theory of this to you but only by doing it can you see how profound the impact is.

At my workshops I get people to take it one step further and go around the room introducing themselves in either physical state, discussing both how they felt and how they perceived others in that state. Next time you feel down rather than just attempt to think happy thoughts, shake it off and adopt the physiology of a champion.

I'VE MISSED MORE THAN 9000 SHOTS IN MY CAREER. I'VE LOST ALMOST 300 GAMES. 26 TIMES, I'VE BEEN TRUSTED TO TAKE THE GAME WINNING SHOT AND MISSED. I'VE FAILED OVER AND OVER AND OVER AGAIN IN MY LIFE. AND THAT IS WHY I SUCCEED.

- MICHAEL JORDAN

CHAPTER 9

Spoilt for Choice

The creator mindset is not only beneficial in restoring sanity and happiness. I actually enjoy looking back when something 'bad' happens and deciphering the role I had to play in it. This way I don't walk away bitter and wounded; I leave having learnt something valuable about life and can adjust future responses accordingly. More often than not, there is actually more to be gained from a 'loss' than a victory. Many sports people say their greatest growth came through loss; it kept them sharp and on top of their game.

I'm not suggesting that we have direct control over the outcome of *everything* that happens in the world. However, we always have choice: a choice in what to do in response to an outcome, and a choice regarding how to feel about it. These are both of paramount importance.

There is *always* choice – this is a view I have refined over many years of conversation and work with those who initially aren't so convinced.

***

We have environmental control, the scale of which is context dependent but the recognition of which is of utmost importance. At one extreme you could say that even with a gun to your head you have choice on what to do or say, but sadly many people throw away their power of choice on the most trivial and mundane things. It's interesting the way people casually throw around words that diminish their responsibility. Unfortunately for those people, I have no qualms in challenging these linguistic violations.

For example: *need* vs *want*. How often could these two be easily (and revealingly) reversed? Too readily we state the *need* for something when in fact it's a *want*. Such a simple word has such a strong bearing on the overall meaning and feeling associated with the sentence.

To clarify; there is not much we *need* in life. Just the simple necessities like good old food, water and oxygen. Anything above the basic level of survival is a *want*. There is a distinct difference in needing oxygen and *needing* to catch a train. Being at the mercy of *need* puts us under an undue amount of stress. Doing something because you *want* to is a lot less effort and equally much more rewarding.

***

We can't always retain full control over the external world.

The internal world on the other hand – that's a different kettle of fish. Picture this; your alarm doesn't go off and you are running late for work. Your car doesn't start, you shell out for a taxi but there's traffic and you sit and watch as the meter clocks up. On top of that you realise your phone hasn't charged and cuts out as you are trying to let the office know you're delayed. It's a roasting hot day and the air con isn't working in the cab. Throw in any other series of unfortunate events to the mix and then ask yourself, *what kind of day are you going to have*?

Whatever day you wish. You see you *always*, absolutely and categorically without a shadow of a doubt, always have the ability to select how you feel.

Don't take my word for it, the quote on the following page is from Viktor Frankl. A Jewish psychiatrist held captive for three years in concentration camps during the Holocaust. A man who suffered inexplicable atrocities at the hands of his Nazi captors and still maintained that one can overcome the greatest of horrors and find happiness. A man whose mother, father, wife and brother died in concentration camps. Makes some of our everyday gripes seem pretty trivial, doesn't it?

EVERYTHING CAN BE TAKEN FROM A MA
BUT ONE THING: THE LAST OF THE HUMA
FREEDOMS - TO CHOOSE ONE'S ATTITUD
IN ANY GIVEN SET OF CIRCUMSTANCES,
TO CHOOSE ONE'S OWN WAY.
- VIKTOR FRANKL

We often hear people state how someone annoys them. More fool them. I can honestly say there is no one on the face of this earth that annoys me; they just don't have that much of a hold on my emotions. *You* are the one who annoys *yourself*. *You* choose how to respond based on your values, beliefs and interpretation of external stimuli.

We don't react to the things that happen to us – we react to the meaning we place upon it.

You're driving the car, stuck in traffic and a car in the right hand lane veers across and pulls in front of you. How do you feel? Can get the blood boiling, can't it? You see this every day; you maybe beep the horn and wave your unfriendly finger at times.

Why? What would cause that to bother you? Did you crash in the scenario? Were you in physical pain? Did you stand to gain anything by getting angry? Whatever the reason you give for getting angry, it's solely down to the meaning *you've* placed upon it. These are merely interpretations of the behaviour with meanings added. Two totally separate things are equated.

The truth is there are a number of reasons this could have happened and a number of meanings you could select to bestow upon a situation like this based on how you want to feel. This links back to what we said earlier on flexibility.

The act is not culpable unless the mind is guilty

Let's break the statement down. It's an interpretation of behaviour, but not forgetting intention. In law, for any crime to be committed there must be the *actus reus* (guilty act) and *mens rea* (guilty mind). So before we play judge, jury and executioner, perhaps we should consider whether we *know* an act was intentional. Have you ever made a mistake driving? I know I have. Did someone beep at you? If so, was that supportive? What response did that elicit from you? If your problem was that the guy (or girl) was rude then is responding by being rude particularly intelligent?

***

Whilst away on a business trip in LA, the PPA team and I were in a car park post spin class and got stuck behind two cars at the exit barrier. The lady in the first car had misplaced her ticket and was having trouble getting out as there were no staff answering the assistance button. Frantically she dashed off in search of a means of exit, leaving her car blocking our only exit. Watching her rush to and from the car we grew frustrated and used a rock, paper, scissors battle to decide who would politely ask the woman to move so that we could leave whilst she found a solution.

My partner Lucy and I were elected as car spokespeople and headed to speak to her. She was away from her vehicle so on the way we stopped at the car in front for a rant and asked if they knew where she had gone.

'I'm not sure,' the lady in front said, 'but I hope she is okay. She seemed very worked up. I think she is late for work and we just don't know what her work situation is.'

We opted to head back to the car, feeling guilty for being annoyed by the incident.

When we returned we relayed the conversation to the guys in the car and laughed as we compared the difference in attitude we held to the lady in front who was more considerate of the first lady's welfare than her own inability to leave the car park. The irony being we were getting worked up to go nowhere, we were on holiday and had no plans for the day other than to relax and enjoy ourselves.

It is now an ongoing joke for us, in our worst American impressions, when someone barges past us or does something we could take offence to – *we just don't know their work situation*.

Empathy is better than anger. Even if the driver isn't as good a driver as you, there is a positive: you are a good driver!

CHAPTER CHALLENGE

TIME TO LET GO

Think of the last interaction you had that really bothered you.

Who was it with?

What happened?

Now drop your pride and write the following:

'I forgive .... because................'

Consider different meanings you could have placed upon the situation. What cover story could you give this person that would lessen your anger? Could you perhaps even see a funny side to what happened if you tried hard enough? Is there anything you could choose to be grateful about?

Buddha once said, 'Holding on to anger is like grasping a hot coal with the intent of throwing it at someone else; you are the one who gets burned.'

Wrong end of the stick

When I was 10 years old, I would go to an after school club some evenings while I waited for my mum to come and pick me up.

One evening we were playing hockey with plastic sticks and an orange rubber puck. We would run up and down in teams and shoot the puck at the old wooden benches turned on their side to score points.

I grew up in Lewisham, so you can imagine that it could get a bit heated at times during these games. In the middle of one game a boy from the year above me, a known trouble maker, walked over and tapped me on the shoulder. I turned to face him.

'Your mum,' he said.

'What?!' I said, a bit caught off guard.

'Your mum,' he repeated bluntly.

Without hesitation I grabbed my hockey stick and struck him on the side of the leg in retaliation. In those days 'your mum' was the ultimate disrespectful statement. He fell to the ground and I raised my stick to strike him again before hearing a familiar voice shouting my name. 'Stephen!' She screamed pulling me away from the young boy. Turning around I saw my mum - *shit*.

'I was just trying to tell you that your mum was there!' whimpered the boy.

When you change the way you look at things, the things you look at change - Wayne Dyer

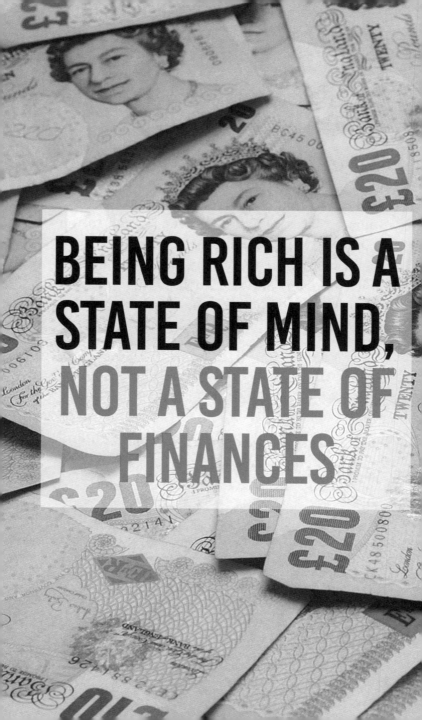

CHAPTER 10

Life balance over bank balance

A standard definition of failure is a lack of success. This would mean that in order for us to truly understand failure we must in fact understand what is meant by its antonym i.e. *success*.

When we think of success we often conjure up images of champagne popping celebrations, achievements of status in a given field and financial accomplishments (to name but a few). The question is, are these true determinants of success or the echo of social conformity? Don't get me wrong, I like champagne and money as much as the next man, but perhaps it is not just about the bubbly and sheets of paper but rather the right we give them to lord over our emotions.

As the saying goes, *money isn't everything but it ranks up there with oxygen* – making the point that lack of money is the real problem, whereas the attempt to amass a surplus isn't a major concern. Money ultimately reflects the resources available to you, no more and no less. It's a tool, a mere means of exchange in the physical realm. And yet it's easy to see how it gets caught up in the great success vs failure debate – so many see it as a measure of achievement.

Saying that money *doesn't* matter would be ignorant. Life is about equilibrium. What matters is the balance between time, money and emotions. The real measurable currency in life is time – the most level playing field that we have. There are 86,400 seconds in a day, and however many of those you spend awake makes a big difference, as we will discuss later. Every day the budget resets and we are greeted with a glowing balance of another 86,400 seconds. The difference then is what you spend that time doing and feeling.

The quality of your life is the quality of your emotions – **Tony Robbins**

That quote is a personal favourite of mine; I've always felt that it sums life up very simply. If you're happy at any given time then your life is good; if you're feeling down, then it isn't (at that point). Simple. This equation happens to negate finances as being directly relevant to the quality of your life. The nearer we can stick to the truth the better – and the only real truth in life is our feelings. You could just as easily be a multi-millionaire who spends their days stressed and upset as a low-paid worker who's happy.

Now to clarify, I'm not saying we should all aim to get a low paid job and whistle while we work. I am saying that reaching financial success without underpinning it with *emotional* success is failure. In order to gain success there are elements beyond the purely financial that are often overlooked. Once they are attended to, then, if it's in line with your values and purpose, by all means make as much money as you wish.

If you took your daily time allowance and monitored yourself across the day you could calculate the amount of time that you spend as a percentage in any given mood. This would demonstrate how much of the day you are happy, for example. We are all human and it would be false for me to propose a utopian idea that people can be happy 100% of the time. That isn't true for a number of reasons. I would be setting you up to fail. The better the percentage though, the better the quality of life.

We are human. Emotions naturally ebb and flow, constantly in a state of flux. It's a modern phenomenon to get sad and look for a quick fix method to solve our problems and popular culture is rife with quick fix solutions to everything. Guess what? It's okay to feel sad from time to time, to just sit within an emotion. Emotions are vital: they are you, and they are telling you something – so tune in! It can actually be nice sometimes to experience sadness, and enjoyable to be angry. Know what it is to be human and have a full spectrum of emotion; just don't stay there or get addicted to these feelings.

Depression is not caused by a lack of anti-depressants. If you are stuck in a negative emotional cycle, solve the problem; covering it up deals (at best) only with the symptoms and (at worst) may hand you a self-identity that'll make it that much harder to shake off negative emotions in the future. The easy way is often not the best. Instead, you need to establish the cause and solve the problem, then develop strategies that will prevent the weeds from returning.

Equally, depression is not caused by a lack of finances. It is paramount to clarify how much money you need and what you want it for – whether it is for things you want to have or do. Then, understand the feeling that having and doing these things will create for you. Continue to work on generating these funds for as long as your target remains the same; and if not, adjust accordingly as plans can change. While on that journey, bear in mind that you can *always* be happy at any moment of that very same journey. Never put happiness off until tomorrow as tomorrow never comes.

CHAPTER 11

So what do you want? And how much of it?

I often bump into people and ask them how they are doing. 'Not bad,' comes the usual reply. Depending on our level of rapport I often take that opportunity to explain that I didn't ask how they are *not* doing. Think about it; why would you say not bad? As pedantic as it may seem, these can ultimately be the subtle distinctions that make all the difference. How you communicate outwardly is more often than not an expression of how you communicate inwardly.

It's futile to focus on the negative. By *negative* I'm not passing a value judgement on what constitutes good and bad; rather, I'm referring to using the *opposite* of something to communicate the meaning of the thing itself. It's futile because the brain will automatically turn its attention to the point of reference. To give you an example if I tell you now **not** to picture a purple kangaroo, the odds are that you will picture a purple kangaroo.

Thus we can understand the struggle of children when a parent tells them very specifically what *not* to do. Don't touch that wall, don't eat those sweets before dinner. The catch is that asking them *not* to do something has in turn focused them on doing precisely that. The art is to redirect thinking towards behaviour or thought processes that are desirable. This is a lot less taxing.

Could the same be true for us? Absolutely! In coaching I have clients tell me all the things that they don't want. I don't want to be broke, I don't want to be hated, I don't want this and I don't want that. 'Great,' I reply, 'so what do you want?' If you don't want to be broke (for example) there is a great deal on the flipside of broke: do you want enough to buy food and pay bills, or enough to holiday four times a year, or enough to buy a jet, or enough to buy a space shuttle?

When delivering training within an organisation in Johannesburg, I managed to get some valuable tourist time. I visited a local attraction called Lion Park, where you are able to interact with various animals. After some time playing with the lion cubs and feeding the giraffe, we set off on a mini safari hosted by Charles (our affable tour guide).

'If you look to your left,' Charles told us, 'you'll see the wildebeest.' Looking over we saw them gathered in all of their glory, savvy creatures by all appearances; but, as Charles explained, 'these animals are very stupid. You see, when they are being chased by lions they look back, and when they look back they don't see where they are going. They get caught. Many wildebeest have been known to even crash into trees during a chase.'

It's hard not to project a metaphor upon this explanation. There are times in our lives when directing our focus poorly can limit our ability to move towards our desired goals. Focusing on what you *do* want and not what you *don't* want may seem obvious, but we often miss the trick.

When finances are low people often focus on the obvious cause – bills or loss of employment, rather than what can be done to improve the situation. This can be a slippery slope.

When we know what it is that we want and what's pivotal to the success of our careers, our lives, and relationships, fantastic things start to happen. We open the doorway to our highest level of awareness. Ideas naturally emerge, we start to easily intuit what to do next. Clarity is brought to our goals and we make more calculated and beneficial decisions. Calmly and purposefully we move in a direction that best serves our purpose. Time, energy and money are not wasted. We focus our thoughts, our actions and our reactions on where they are required.

So be careful what you focus on – because you might just get it!

CHAPTER CHALLENGE

TARGET PRACTICE

Get into the habit of stating what you *do* over what you *don't*. Be specific. How much of it do you want? How will you know when you have reached that goal?

Set 3 positive goals:

- 1 month goal

- 3 month goal

- 12 month goal

ON'T BELIEVE EVERYTHING YOU THINK

BYRON KATIE

CHAPTER 12

F.E.A.R. False Evidence Appearing Real

Everything you want is on the other side of fear - **Jack Canfield**

There are only two innate fears that we have from birth: the fear of loud noises and the fear of falling. These are likely engrained in us as survival mechanisms. The rest we inherit through the course of our lives (and interestingly we tend to share the same fears); fear of being rejected and fear of not being good enough tend to rank highest on the list. Most other fears can be routed back to these.

In between what happens and the interpretation of our 'natural' response lies the opportunity to change our lives.

In 2015 I was a semi-finalist on a TV programme called *Special Forces: Ultimate Hell Week*. Shot in the Brecon Beacons (the training ground of the British SAS), the series pitted 'the fittest men and women' against 'the toughest challenge of their lives'. The aim was to push each contestant's mental and physical strength to the limit. As a recruit on the show I suffered some of the most unbearable physical anguish of my entire life.

The show was specially constructed to reflect the Special Forces' selection and training from around the world. Every two days a different nation was in charge of destroying what was left of the 30 original recruits that had begun on Day 1. The US Navy SEALs, the Philippine's NAVSOG (Naval Special Operations Group), the Australian SAS, the Israeli Counter Terrorism, the Russian Spetsnaz and the UK's SAS took it in turn to put us into a world of suffering in order to separate the weak from the strong.

On the morning of Day 9, in his opening speech, the Officer representing the Russian Spetsnaz told us that we must face our fears. I have no problem with this concept; although fear is no more than a concept, I can recognise the positive intention behind the proposal. The difficulty arose when, at the verge of a cliff before abseiling down, I was asked "What are you afraid of?" Instantly I knew this would spell the beginning of the end for my position on the TV show.

On the one hand I could play the game and proclaim to hold a regular fear of spiders, heights or perhaps death – but this would be at the sacrifice of my integrity and also everything that I stand for (as you've seen so far in this book). I answered with the truth.

"I have no fears Sir".

Not intending to undermine the fundamental aims of the process we were engaged in, I presented my justification in the most amicable and non-challenging way I could by going on to say that, "I believe fear is a choice". The next two days were tipped to be long ones (as the theme was fear).

I was repeatedly invited over the duration of the two days to reconsider my position on this matter and, apologetically, I expressed my inability to do so. At 3am on the second day, we were woken up and told one by one to lay in a bathtub filled with blood and body parts. Lined up in front of the tub the Officer asked, "Who here has no fear?" It was clear this was to single me out. Slowly and reluctantly I raised my hand.

"Me, Sir." I knew I had been set up. I was left until last when everyone had gone in to clean up. Whilst laying in the tub, the Russian came over to me, cameras rolling, and leaning over he asked me once more if I was willing to concede. Again I told him *no* (in the nicest way I could).

After cleaning up and going back to sleep, we were woken up again shortly after 4am. This time I was made to bathe in offal alone. Did it make me scared? No. Concerned about the risk of infection to the multiple wounds we had gained over the ten days, but not enough for me to speak out of turn. I processed those thoughts in silence. Recognising danger and feeling fear are two very different things.

Midway through Day 10 we were blindfolded, put in a Land Rover and told not to speak. We sat in silence, but it didn't faze me. What would be the sense in worrying about what isn't or what could be? Why care about what *hasn't* happened? Mindfulness and being present are such fantastic tools in maintaining happiness; in that given moment I was absolutely fine, safe, well and comfortable. I began to look for a positive. I found one fast; I was beyond relieved to not be doing another physical activity after ten days of relentless 'beasting' – the time spent in the Land Rover was a welcome rest. We arrived at the destination and were told to get out and led to wooden stumps upon which we were seated.

"Watch him," a voice commanded. That's when the attack dogs began to growl. Still I was uninjured and therefore undisturbed. Sensory deprivation is a fabulous tool for relaxation. We were then made to put a bandage on our leg, blindfolded, whilst the attack dogs barked next to our faces. This was after having oil sprayed on our hands to make it more difficult to open the packaging.

We were then led one by one for an interview with the Russian. We ran in circles around my beliefs again, and he then told me how we had all failed. We'd been set up to fail from the start; the task itself was to relay information played over a speaker drowned out by the barking of the dogs whilst applying the wound dressing. "Sometimes you win and sometimes you learn," he said. The two things aren't that different; in fact, given the choice, I would rather learn than 'win'.

Ultimately the two days with the Russian resulted in my being asked to leave the programme at the end of Day 10. In my leaving interview I was asked by Freddy Flintoff how it felt to leave having been a strong contender to win. "Oh I definitely won," I explained. "I have learned more about myself than ever before. I have trained alongside the world's most elite Special Forces. I have met and suffered side by side with some of the most inspirational people I could have ever imagined and I was asked to leave because of my integrity, not through lack of physical or mental ability. That's a *major* win. In fact everyone who is still there now is a winner in their own right." Freddy smiled, I guess there's not much you can reply to that.

Walking away I was proud to have protected my moral standing although I couldn't help but feel this to be somewhat a Pyrrhic victory and it prompted me to think this over in greater depth. Fear is certainly a decision; it is my job as a coach and trainer to teach others that in spite of what our external world presents to us we always have an influence on the state of mind that we allow it to elicit.

It's paramount to consider carefully the label you place upon the internal feelings you experience in response to external stimuli. As an example: you are standing at the doorway of an aeroplane preparing to jump, your heart is beating rapidly, your breathing is shallow and your palms are sweaty. You naturally decide to interpret this feeling as *fear*.

Before you are so quick to condemn yourself, think again; is there a time in life when your body may present you with the same physiological responses but instead the emotion is different, perhaps even a positive one. How about excitement? By labelling this response as excitement rather than terror, we've made a choice that allows us to elicit a different and more beneficial emotion from that same initial feeling. This is the difference between an adrenaline junkie and a nervous wreck; labels come at a high price. Maintain conscious awareness when interpreting your own state; don't confuse ability to assess danger with fear and learn to love your body's responses – they are there to serve you.

***

I do a physical demonstration of this in my public speaking workshops. I ask people to stand in one of three groups to denote their level of comfort with regard to public speaking.

The scenario is you are asked to give a presentation to 500 people on the subject of your choice but with only one hour to prepare.

I then allocate three areas within the room and ask delegates to physically stand in the area that best relates to them in the given situation – comfortable, stretched or panicked. Amidst our comfort zone discussion I pose the question to the people in the panic zone, *how do you know that you are panicking*? To get as close to the truth as possible, I push for answers specific to their body's physiological responses. Heart racing, butterflies in stomach, breathing rate and depth changes, palms sweating and body temperatures lifting, for example.

At this point I would like to remind you of our calibration versus interpretation chat. The physiological responses are factual and therefore calibration but the belief that this feeling means one is afraid is what? You got it – interpretation.

I head across to the guys in the comfort zone and ask them, *do any of you guys get these responses*? They usually say yes, and so we explore what then makes the difference. The answer is the *interpretation*; what they are choosing to label this state as, then move on to experience. People in the comfort zone experiencing the same response will brand it as excitement, 'buzzing' or simply being in a peak performance state; those in the panic zone might say fear, panic or even terror.

Essentially it's the same response! The solace for us is in the fact that when we become consciously aware of this we can select the interpretation that best suits us, or as I often do, simply recognise the shift internally and place no judgement on it. This is a more mindful approach; neither way is right or wrong, it's whatever works for you.

If we delve deeper we can see that as ever there is a positive intent from the body in producing the response that it does.

When I take my 'Live Daily' groups canyoning in Spain I explain that it is not the act of jumping off the cliff that scares them – it is the physiological response to the prospect of doing it. The closer we can get to the truth the more scope we have to influence the outcome of a situation. To be philosophical and paraphrase Descartes, we know only what we think. In dealing with challenges it is important to keep in touch with our true feelings. Failing to do so will drastically limit our capability of truly overcoming the challenge.

CHAPTER CHALLENGE

FEARLESS FRIENDLINESS

As we discussed earlier, the fear of rejection is one of our most prevalent fears. It is also one of the most debilitating fears we suffer. Many people never live to their full potential for fear of being rejected when the truth is they could have been revered for stepping into their greatness. So – let's step into yours.

For this challenge you will need to be in public. The perfect location is one where people are sat or stood still (and can't escape you). Trains, tubes, coffee shops are ideal examples. Approach five different people and introduce yourself. Make sure you smile on approach. Tell them your name and let them know you just like to say hello to people.

Note: this is not pick-up training nor sales. **Do not** hold an agenda of any description and let this be transparent. After small talk bid them farewell and keep it moving. No contact exchange, just a hello for hello's sake.

Notice in comparison to your prior nerves about this challenge how well received you were. If you did have any odd interactions, consider the humour in them. Consider also whether the person on the other end of the conversation may have been more nervous than you. They too more than likely have the same fear of rejection (unless they have read this book before you, of course).

CHAPTER 13

Smokescreens

We often throw up an internal smokescreen that disables our ability to truly interpret our own feelings. In 1894 Sigmund Freud spoke of *free-floating anxiety* – a type of anxiety caused by internal conflict. He suggested that we are only *truly* aware of the feeling of anxiety and we then invoke a seemingly logical reason to explain why we feel the way we do.

In my work I have found this to be the case with at least 90% of my clients. They tend to explain why one thing is making them feel a certain way and only later realise that they were a far cry from the truth. Feelings are the purest thing available to us; misinterpretation of them is dangerous.

I recently coached a young man on the cusp of building his singing career. We sat and discussed where he wanted to be and who he would need to become in order to realise his dream. He told me how he saw himself up early and working hard on his passion. We planned an average day and then an average week. In order to do all he wanted to he was up at 6am and would turn in at 11pm when finished, working through weekends. With conviction and tenacity he explained there was no time to rest in pursuit of this goal and no time to waste.

Aware that he was potentially setting himself up to fail, I asked if this would make him happy. He explained that happiness would come after the work is done. So, I changed my approach and asked whether or not he would be able to sustain this level of work without rest factored in. He thought about it and then proposed to rest one evening during the week and half a day at the weekend.

I changed my approach and drew out another piece of paper, asking him to write down five of his values (one's judgement of what is important in life). Due to the intense state he was in I expected them to be along the lines of *work*, *drive*, *progress*, *significance* and *success*.

Instead, he replied without hesitation: "Well, this is going to sound silly given what I just said but happiness." As we know, this is our primary aim in life. We discussed the ecology of the week template around this value.

Then I asked for another value. "Family," he responded, again without hesitation. His state had visibly changed; he breathed out and relaxed comfortably into the room. I reached over and shook his hand smiling, "It's nice to finally meet you," I said aware that the past half an hour had been an array of smoke screens.

"Give me a third." He looked down and started crying. This is always tough for me but I waited in silence as through floods of tears he finally processed his own truths. As humans we are hard wired to be empathetic and at moments like these we tend to intervene and deny someone the opportunity to face their intrinsic reality. Eventually he looked up, "Humanity." He went on to explain that this value included love and respect. Number four was *life*, which for him meant both awareness of the reality of death and the sanctity of life; and, finally, *unity*. Then I pushed for one more, bonus value: "Freedom," he said, still wiping his face. We spoke about what freedom meant to him.

I drew yet another sheet of paper. "What would a typical day look like that is in line with these values?" As you can imagine this was nothing like the one we mapped before. This one had very visual descriptions; he was already living there in his mind. "First, I would do something that I don't ever usually do," he beamed. "I would have breakfast." After describing the exact breakfast he told me how he would go for a morning walk and then work on his own business that was in line with his values and factor in plenty of time to see family, totally absent from his former plan. Then he went to speak and again burst into tears, "If I could have this life, I don't care if anyone ever hears me sing again."

I'm not the first coach this person had visited but they didn't see what I saw. He had been presenting the problem and the previous coaches had been kindly working hard on creating solutions and plans to achieve what he said he wanted. The reason this wasn't working is because what he said he wanted, wasn't what he truly wanted. I call this being out of alignment, when your unconscious is out of line with your conscious. We will immediately self-sabotage a plan that doesn't account for the wants of the unconscious mind.

Since this initial session he has never stopped thanking me. Later on we built a dream that was more ecologically viable, included singing and ran parallel to his values. This is why I do what I do; it's in line with my values.

CHAPTER CHALLENGE

CHECK YOUR TRACKING

Did you think you could walk away from this chapter like that?

No way!

It's your time to check your tracking. List 5 of your values. There are no right or wrong answers. Be careful not to overthink what is meant by value, just put whatever comes to mind. The more you have to think about it, the less true it is.

Once you have all 5, add one more. These 6 values define who you are; they are also your answer to what to do. When making decisions refer back to these and consider how those decisions line up with your values.

Write these values up neatly and read them every morning when you wake up and every evening when you go to bed. Some of my clients keep a small card in their wallets to keep them primed throughout the day. Don't read them and then overthink them, just read them to be aware of them. This will keep your RAS primed and on the lookout for opportunities to align with your values.

A simple few seconds in the morning and evening that will without a shadow of a doubt change your life. If you feel at any point along the way one or more of the values change then amend them accordingly. You are a free agent and can adapt.

BUT
NOTHING

CHAPTER 14

The 'but' flip

Allow me to share with you a fantastic technique to quickly turn around a negative sentence into a positive sentence. It works on yourself or can work when communicating with somebody else. The end of a 'but' sentence is always strongest so a subtle change in syntax can change the meaning and thus result of the sentence. I could say *the man stroked the cat* or I could say *the cat stroked the man,* the words are the same but the order and sequence has changed – and the meaning has drastically altered.

So, I might say to myself,

*I really want to go to the gym today **but** it's raining.*

The 'but' here is an excuse as to why I'm not going to do what I do actually want to do. In

133

order to flip it I keep the same words and change the order:

*It's raining **but** I really want to go to the gym today.*

Notice straight away there's a totally different flow to that sentence. In the former we saw the negative close off the sentence and the possibility for growth and then in the latter we can see the power shift from the negative to the positive part of the statement. To make this stronger we now add a 'because' on to the end of it. It then sounds a little bit like this:

*It's raining **but** I really want to go to the gym today **because** I value my health.*

The 'because' serves to strengthen the second part of the sentence. This is a powerful exercise used on oneself and can be subtly used to positively influence others.

I may catch someone offering me a 'but' sentence such as *I want to start my own business **but** I don't have much money.* To give this person their power back I would subtly flip it and repeat it. *Okay, so you don't have much money*

but _you want to start a business._ Read those two sentences and notice the difference. As I have used their exact words there's nothing they can really question about it. I would continue that by asking what the next step might be as we are now working on a solution not a problem.

***

'But' is also a favourite tool of the dream stealer ('but-heads'). _I like your idea but *insert bullshit negative statement here*._ These are basically 'yes buts', which is clearly a contradiction in itself – how can an answer ever be 'yes but'? It can be yes, it can be no, it can even be I don't know. It absolutely cannot be 'yes but'. This is quite simply a masquerading 'No.'

So how do we rectify this verbal mess? One solution was presented to me by Maurice DeCastro who told me how he banned the use of the word 'but' within a company he was working with, instead replacing it with the word 'and.' This meant that in any meetings people were not able to shut others down; a response was then able to add value and create opportunity rather than stifling possibility for growth.

Before: 'Yes, but we would have to work out how to get that approved.'

After: 'Yes, and we would have to work out how to get that approved.'

Now we are adding value rather than taking away, we are looking for ways to make it happen (not stop it happening). Maurice went one step further by introducing rubber balls with the word 'and' printed on them, distributing them throughout the workforce. Each time someone slipped up they would quickly have a hailstorm of *AND* balls coming their way.

I adopted the same strategy within my company Fury MMA. It seemed we had a phase when every idea presented was shot down and as a result the company was struggling to grow and progress. The solution then, was to get rid of the but-heads. We adopted the 'Yes and' strategy and I can say from first-hand experience the positive effects on the business were profound. It was one of the most fruitful and exciting times for the business. Ideas would seem to get out of hand, only for us to realise that nothing was in fact out of hand – we generated some amazing ideas that led us to host our best events to date.

CHAPTER CHALLENGE

IT'S TIME TO FLIP YOUR BUT

1. Write a sentence out that you would have previously used a 'but' in. Aim for your go-to excuse for not making something happen.

2. Read the sentence out loud, noticing how it feels.

3. Flip the sentence in your head and repeat it.

4. Notice the difference.

5. Now switch the 'but' for 'and' and notice the difference again.

6. Write this new improved sentence down.

7. Read it out loud and feel the difference.

8. Now add the 'because' to the sentence.

9. Make this your new default sentence in relation to this matter.

ALL OF OUR DREAMS CAN COME TRUE,
IF WE HAVE THE COURAGE TO PURSUE THEM

WALT DISNEY

The Disney Creativity Strategy

Disney has an amazing strategy when it comes to innovation and growth. When brainstorming ideas they use a different room for each stage to physically differentiate the phases with environments conducive to the theme.

The three phases of creative planning:

Dreamer

In this phase they set out to ascertain *what* specifically they want to achieve, taking into account the reasons why. The Dreamer Room contains inspirational quotes and drawings on the wall. They don't consider any potential obstacles; instead, they open their minds to what they want and where it will subsequently get them. Ideas are shared and not brought down, nobody is permitted to naysay whilst in dreamer phase – they allow ideas to run wild and free.

Realist

In this phase they consider *how* specifically the idea(s) can be implemented. This room has tools and instruments that facilitate the manifestation of the dreams. Storyboards are drafted containing the content from the Dreamer phase. They ask what will be required to make it work, who will be responsible for it and what resources they will need. This phase is centred on building a strategy. It was not a time for holes to be picked, rather for a tangible game plan to be introduced.

Critic

In this phase they begin to look at *why* the idea may not work out. The room used is often referred to as the 'sweatbox' due to its location underneath the staircase. The ecology of the plan is considered. Does the intention match the strategy? Objections to the ideas are raised and discussed. Only the ideas are criticised, reviewed and evaluated and never the individual behind an idea. They consider who is affected by the idea and how. Finally when and where will they not want to see the idea implemented?

CHAPTER 15

Honesty over modesty

There is nothing enlightened about shrinking so that other people will not feel insecure around you...as we let our own light shine, we unconsciously give others permission to do the same – **Marianne Williamson**

In today's society we are often encouraged to 'be humble'. When was the last time you stopped and considered the implications of this? Just because someone has made a pretty square with a quote and posted it on Instagram or some other form of *unsociable* media, it doesn't make it a valid life strategy. It's more likely to be a passive aggressive attempt to chastise those who offer them a mirror to their own insecurities. If Muhammad Ali didn't say that he was the greatest, *would* he have been the greatest? Without truly embodying that belief, *could* he have been the greatest?

How did Muhammad Ali achieve what he did? Well he trained harder than most and performed better than them on the night too, that's for sure. Although, as we know, boxing matches are not confined entirely to the ring nor is becoming a marketable and profitable athlete. Ali was renowned for the sharp wit he used to dance around his opponents and jab at their psyche long before their feet ever stepped on the canvas.

He would make a rather bold public declaration prior to proving it, that he was '*the greatest*'. This had two major benefits. One: it influenced his opponent's thinking. It planted doubt, which gave Ali a stronger chance to win. Even if the opponent didn't doubt their own ability they would often become emotionally riled and want to prove him wrong which affected their decision making and brought them out of their usual style, leaving enough holes in their game for Ali to capitalise on. Two: it allowed him to believe in himself and therefore access the resources needed to complete the task.

Ali's example begs the question: what's the difference between confidence and arrogance? The difference is subjective opinion. It's not truth. If I consider somebody to be arrogant, that's solely my perception. It's likely that I'm perceiving something I want (or at least admire) and on some underlying level I'm jealous, whether I realise it or not – or I'm allowing somebody's behaviour to offend me, which is foolish. Why would I allow anybody control over my emotions?

I put arrogance in the same folder as the Tooth Fairy. Some people are confident and some people are rude. Arrogance is when confidence is combined with rudeness or poor communication skills. Take Kanye West – the man is very confident but he's *competent* too. What rubs people up the wrong way is his rudeness and lack of communication skills. Muhammad Ali was an elegant communicator, speaking in poetry and humour. In fact, when confidence is communicated well, we don't call it arrogance – we call it charisma.

There's a lot to be learned from the study of confidence and arrogance. It's an interesting debate. You should be highly confident, the challenge is that we're worried about being perceived as arrogant. Yet if we don't speak our confidence into the world, then we can't access the same level of self-belief. When people climb to a certain level, others want to pull them down (we'll talk about this *crab bucket mentality* later). If you start to feel somebody is arrogant, then consider what it is within you that is causing that feeling.

So, arrogance is bullshit. Rudeness is one thing, but confidence is an attribute. Be openly confident and encourage others to be confident too.

CHAPTER CHALLENGE

SPEAK NOW OR FOREVER HOLD YOURSELF BACK

Stop now and just repeat a sentence 10 times. Make it a positive sentence. Make it light-hearted if you please, for example; *I am extremely good-looking*. Say it 10 times. *I am extremely good-looking. I am extremely good-looking. I am extremely good-looking*. Notice a smile spreading across your face, you'll find a different feeling coming out of your body because you say it and it becomes so. And when you feel better looking, guess what? You'll look better looking.

Alternatively, keep it simple and say to yourself, *I am the greatest*. What's a minute every day just to let yourself know that you're the greatest? There's enough diversity in this world that we can all be the greatest in something; you might be the greatest in making fireplaces or the greatest at designing biscuits. If you aim to be the greatest, you're a lot more likely to get there than if you aim for mediocrity.

IT IS FAR BETTER TO BE ALONE
THAN TO BE IN BAD COMPANY

GEORGE WASHINGTON

CHAPTER 16

Have you got crabs?

Crabs are rife. I for one can come out on a limb here and say I have suffered from crabs in the past. It is important that you understand both how you recognise if you have crabs and also how to get rid of them.

In Filipino culture they speak of something called the *crab bucket mentality.* If you put a crab in a bucket, then the crab will undoubtedly climb out to freedom. That is perfectly normal behaviour. If you put a cast of crabs in a bucket, however, then as soon as one crab tries to get out the others will pull it back down. *We're not getting out, so you're not getting out either.*

Our mentality is often exactly the same. It seems that there are many groups of human crabs who appear when one person tries to better themselves, trying to pull them back down when they step out and take their life to the next level.

When I was 18 I decided to pursue my dream job and apply to be a firefighter for the London Fire Brigade. I wanted to become the hero I had always dreamed of being (after my brief stint as a lifeguard hadn't turned out to be the Baywatch I had hoped for). The day that I turned around and shared this goal I was met with pessimism and doubt. There were 10,000 people at the time applying for 50 jobs, many from other brigades or services – and then me, at the time working as a delivery driver for Pizza Hut. Great, I had nothing to lose and a lot to gain.

The test process was extensive, spanning a 12 month period. We had an in depth application, 4 written tests, 11 fitness and strength tests, several work related tests, psychological profiling, medical tests and reports, references, observed group exercises and eventually, if you passed each of those phases you had an interview. Long story short - I got the job. And I took a great deal of pleasure in proving the many naysayers wrong.

This love for going against the grain of peer expectations has been a recurrent theme throughout my life. The earliest reference I have is one my beloved Mum takes much pride in telling people. At six years old she would take me to swimming lessons, in which you could work towards different certificates and badges.

I immediately sought out the top badge that required a 2000m swim and stated to my instructor that I wished to complete it. He laughed and said I was welcome to try, believing that it wasn't possible that my scrawny self would be able to swim over a mile continuously without touching the side of the pool.

My Mum laughs now whenever she tells the story. She recalls warning him, "If he says he'll do it, he'll do it," before sitting down with her book, occasionally looking up to see my toothless grin bobbing up and down in the pool. I swam my little heart out, for what seemed like an eternity, until eventually I reached the 2km target.

Jealousy is just love and hate at the same time
- Drake

This crab bucket mentality can be caused by jealousy. Jealousy is a fantastic waste of energy. Internally we interpret jealousy to mean that we don't like an individual. Truth be told, you often dislike them because they are displaying a quality or trait that you *do* like. It's an interesting anomaly. If it was something that was of no interest to you then you invariably wouldn't even recognise the trait to start with, least of all feed it your attention. If you have no interest in fishing you would not be jealous of someone at work who is a top-level fisherman with all of the top end equipment and a track record of catching some great whoppers. You simply wouldn't care.

Jealousy comes at a price. The moment you cast hate onto an attribute or characteristic that someone is displaying you shut down your ability to recreate the same within your own life. You would cause an internal conflict the moment you began to strive for that characteristic or attribute. One part of your brain would be telling you to go for it whereas another would be relating your behaviour to whatever undesirable aspersions you cast upon it.

The key to utilising the state lies in disabling the hate and concentrating your focus onto what it is that you love about what that person is doing. Where focus goes, energy flows. Recognise what it is that they are doing well; recognise what it is inside you that is reacting. Jealousy is best treated as a trigger to take action and get moving in some area where you want to make progress. When I feel overwhelmed or behind on something I remember the Zig Ziglar quote: "you don't have to be great to start but you have to start to be great.'

Once the hate is eradicated you must be supportive, whether overtly or just inside your own mind. In order to succeed in life, I truly believe it is essential to wish for others to be successful too. Secondly, be grateful to this person that they have given you the wake up call to realise your potential. If you can see something in someone then you can have it, remember? Simple as that. The fact that they have given you this reminder could be the greatest gift you could get, a push to overcome inertia and get you moving towards your goals.

Ask them how they do what they do. Congratulate them and ask how they get the results they do. This is applicable to all circumstances, whether it's a couple who seem to be happier than you in their relationship or someone performing better than you at work. If you wish to replicate their results then you have to first understand their strategies. I do this by asking successful people from different fields how they do what they do.

What I find when doing this is that most people are really happy to share their methods; effectively it's a compliment when someone asks you how to do something that you are doing well. What is very interesting is that people who are achieving in life will readily disclose how they have created the life they have; those that are failing will quickly tell you how it's not their fault and their lack of success is out of their control.

Whenever someone acts like a crab and starts pulling you down, thank them and continue as planned. Use the criticism and negativity as fuel to drive your will to succeed in whatever the task may be. Before you take it to heart do remember that it's often just that they love you, they care about you and they don't want you to get hurt, and thus that's the best advice they feel they can give. What is important to do in all instances is to trust your intuition. If you feel that the bucket needs to be climbed out of, then do it!

Support others, push them, help them to find and develop their dream rather than pulling one another back down. As we are all in this bucket called life together.

CHAPTER CHALLENGE

DESTROY THOSE CRABS

It is time to look into your own social circle and consider who is around you. When you've decided to do something different to what you're normally doing or tried to elevate yourself, what's the response from those around you? Have you ever noticed that people tried to pull you back down? Are you surrounded by friends that are going to help push you to the next level in life – or are you surrounded by crabs?

Over the next 10 days I challenge you to no longer be a crab. Support everyone around you, even if you don't fully believe in what they say. Bite your tongue when you feel critical. Find the crabs in your own life and eradicate them – they are of no use to you. Don't let yourself be held back, and equally never hold anyone else back. Treat those crabs immediately!

CHAPTER 17

Good for nothing

Being good for nothing (being good without the expectation of any reward), is a true measurement of one's greatness.

When I am driving, for example, I am always an extremely courteous driver; I let people go and thank other drivers profusely when they are kind to me. One day I caught myself muttering when I let someone go and they neglected to say thanks. Immediately I recognised this shift into negativity and stopped to consider the root cause of it. I pondered my intention when letting the car go; I wanted to help someone's day go by a bit easier. I considered the outcome against my intention, they matched up well.

My problem then? I clearly harboured some level of expectation that this person should or at least would say thanks. When they didn't, I chose to take offence. It would seem in this small scale example that I was being nice with the expectation of getting something back – albeit a small thing but a thing none the less. Hence I wasn't being good for nothing.

The beauty of selfless giving is to truly give without any expectation of receiving, to remove your 'self' from the equation. If I revisit the example I gave, there are a multitude of reasons the driver may have neglected to say thank you (including that they did and I never actually saw it). Bottom of the pile is the possibility that they were rude. Either way if my intention was unselfish then I would give regardless.

Walking to meet a friend once I noticed a parking ticket sat on a car's windscreen. My heart sank, drivers reading this will know the pain these little pieces of paper can cause. In a bid to be good for nothing I decided to put the money for the ticket in with the ticket accompanied by a note that read: 'Saw this parking ticket and didn't want it to ruin your day. £60 enclosed. Have a good one.' I sat a distance away and watched the lady's reaction as she read the note and found the money. I said nothing to her but walked away with a smile, knowing that I had made her happy. It can be that easy to make someone's day.

I have done a lot of work with young people in schools, young offender institutes and pupil referral units. Primarily I work with those with behavioural difficulties, relating well having been a bit of a firecracker myself when growing up. One project I worked on recently was to incentivise young people to perform better. We decided to create a scheme where students are rewarded with things such as trips.

One of the teachers was adamant that we give rewards to the students that performed well in their studies, whether it was through grades or just effort such as attendance. I disagreed immediately. What about the ones who don't perform well or make an effort? *They don't deserve it,* chimed in the other teachers. Wrong. The more challenged the student is the less likely they'll be to perform well and the more likely that they will then slip through the net. The more challenged the student, the more *necessary* the attention.

What if we just gave them the rewards with no expectation of anything back? I suggested. A lot of the young people we were dealing with felt that no one cared. The only way to truly reach them was not to be manipulative or attempt to dangle carrots in order to change the superficial level behaviour, but rather shatter their beliefs that people don't care and instil a new one – that some people are *good for nothing*. In order to break up their behavioural patterns we had to interrupt their current cycle of thinking, to change *you're naughty and you're told off* to *you're naughty and I still love you.*

There is a great book by Ken Blanchard called *Whale Done*. He speaks of how they use only positive reinforcements and no punishment to train orcas in SeaWorld. Leaving ethical considerations of captivation of killer whales aside for a moment, the point that you can encourage behaviour in the absence of punishment is profound. How would you even attempt to punish a killer whale? The book reverses the usual paradigm and speaks of catching people doing things right as opposed to doing things wrong. It focuses on redirecting negative behaviour or not responding to it and affirming only the good.

The challenge we had to overcome with the unit was that some of the young people were totally devoid of what could be labelled good behaviour so there was nothing to reinforce. To change a belief you must first introduce doubt into the equation and once doubt exists you can expand it and eventually transition to the new belief. This new approach created breakthroughs unlike any before within the referral unit and has since become a staple of the school's ethos.

Only when we truly give of ourselves can we reasonably expect to see anything back. **In order to multiply your happiness you must first divide it.**

CHAPTER CHALLENGE

BE GOOD FOR NOTHING

Your challenge for this chapter is to do something nice for someone. Great or small, do it – and don't let them know that you were behind it. I now integrate this as a practice every week and can honestly say nothing I do is much more rewarding. You don't have to do anything huge. Notice the way you feel when you do it.

If you really can't think of someone that could benefit from your help then volunteer your time. Pop into a retirement home for a chin wag, help out at the local charity shop or donate your time to an animal rescue shelter.

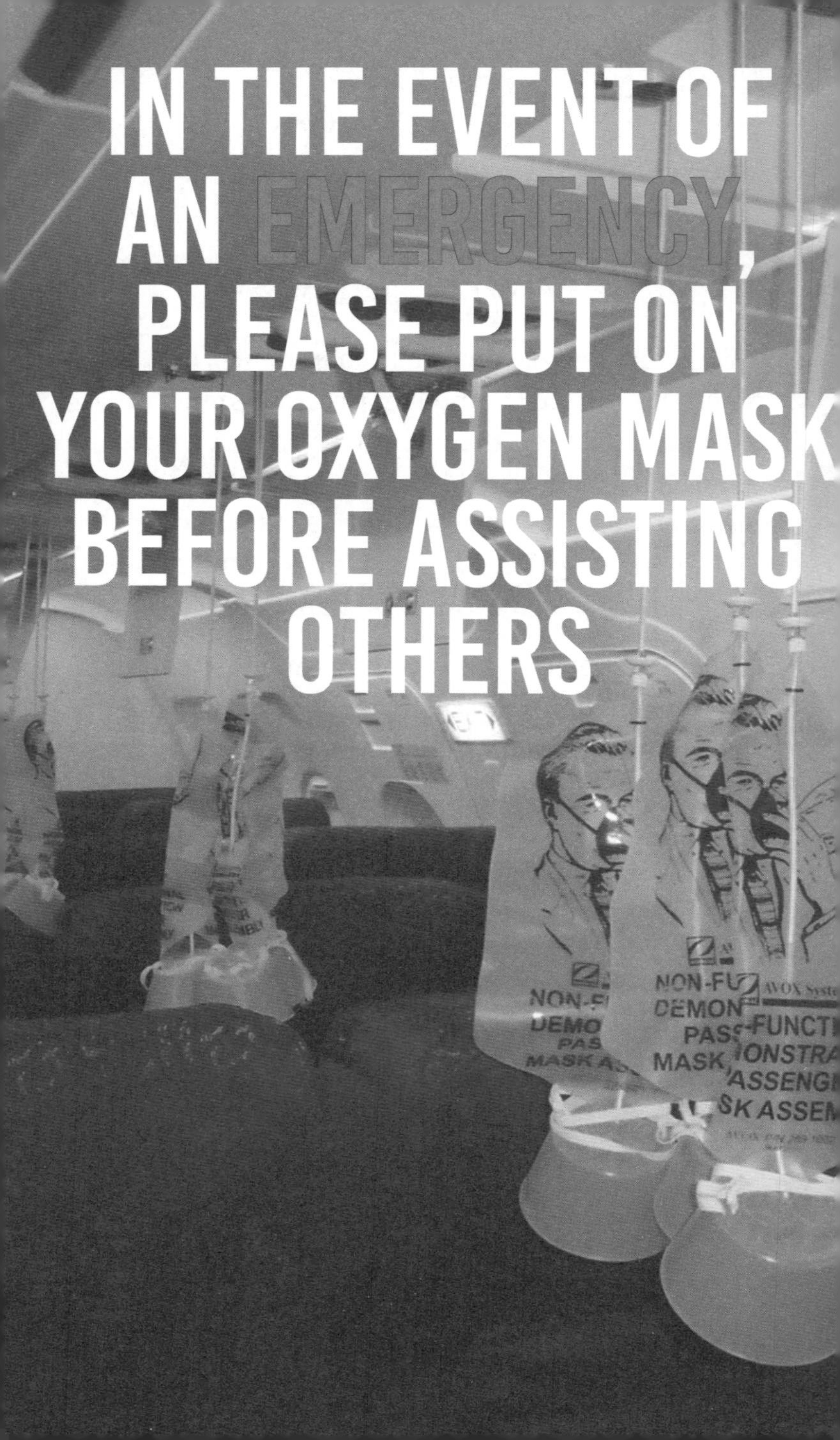
IN THE EVENT OF
AN EMERGENCY,
PLEASE PUT ON
YOUR OXYGEN MASK
BEFORE ASSISTING
OTHERS

CHAPTER 18

You have to be selfish to be selfless

As a frequent flyer, I am often subject to the pre-flight safety announcements. As much as they don't rock my world, there was one statement that recently stood out to me. Although I had heard it time and time again, this time it took on a different meaning; 'In the event of an emergency, please put on your oxygen mask before assisting others.' A seemingly logical proposition perhaps – but common sense is sadly not always common practice.

The reality is that they say this for a reason. If the plane were to lose air pressure for some bizarre reason and the oxygen masks were to actually drop, a lot of parents would likely grab at masks and heroically tend to their young before turning their attention to their own needs. You might think it is the *right* thing to do;

you, however, are of a great deal more value as a hero that *can* breathe than one that can't.

This was the same when I was a firefighter. We didn't get to a fire and decide that the situation was so critical that we had to run in without donning our breathing apparatus. Why? Because we would have only been increasing the casualty count, not helping the situation. So the question is why in life do we not follow the same protocol? *What makes us think we can save others before we have taken care of ourselves?*

Of course the urge to do this comes from a good place. The intention is pure but the action and the intention don't match and so the desired outcome is often missed. The reality is that *in order to be selfless, you must first be selfish*. By that I mean you can't cure world hunger if you can't even adequately feed yourself. It is okay to look after number one – in fact, it's essential!

I'm being a touch pedantic but what I'm really referring to is self-care, which I will discuss later in this chapter. Being selfish and self-care are two very different things: self-care is looking after your needs, but being selfish is looking after your needs and not caring about others. You can actually care about others way before you are able to physically do anything for them and that's okay. It's not selfish, it's sensible.

As a psychotherapist I see this all too often; therapists are treating clients when they haven't yet overcome their own challenges. Besides being incongruent, it's irresponsible. Much like a recovery driver coming to tow a broken down vehicle when he hasn't filled his own tank up before leaving.

Relationships are a prime example of something that cannot thrive without self-care. If you haven't taken the time to love yourself, then it is fatuous to assume you are able to love another. A healthy relationship will only occur when two people are happy with themselves first. Without this fundamental base you can virtually guarantee a world of trouble ahead whether through jealousy, insecurity, distrust, miscommunication or otherwise.

A relationship, at its purest, is the epitome of selflessness and isn't just meant to make you happy; your duty within the relationship is *solely* to make your spouse happy. How well you do this will be dependent on your own level of happiness beyond the relationship. The happiness you ultimately receive from the relationship itself comes from the happiness you create in another; that is *true* love.

***

So what do we need to do to care for ourselves? We need to operate in a *peak performance state* – and in order to do that we need to address both our physical needs and our emotional needs. Sleep, food and shelter, and the resource to allow these things to be possible (in today's society that can often equate to some degree of finances). Last but not least, we need to take care of our emotional needs.

"I'm happy to help," we often say. Indeed you must *be* happy in order *to* help; you are not much help when you're miserable. Take the time to look after your own needs, meditate, relax, listen to music and enjoy life a bit. Know that there will always be things to do and you will never be able to do them well if you are not in a peak performance state – and that means looking after your own needs first.

How many times have you promised the world and delivered exactly nothing?

The key is not to let your mouth write cheques that your butt can't cash. Think realistically when committing to something about the reality of carrying it out. I live by this ethos: **under**-promise and **over**-deliver. This earns respect and credibility as opposed to those who do the converse and lose integrity and opportunities.

It's always tempting as a *nice* person to commit to things before realising they are unachievable or even sometimes knowing they are. This is actually not being a *nice* person at all – it's being a timewaster and a liar. Being nice is being true to yourself, and to others.

CHAPTER CHALLENGE

RESTORING THE EQUILIBRIUM

Create a list of 10 things you enjoy doing that have no negative consequences or side effects. You can put down yoga or reading but don't put going to the pub for a drink. The first purpose of this challenge is to clarify what it is that you actually enjoy doing; not what your husband enjoys doing, not what your friends enjoy doing but what *you* enjoy. An alarming number of people really struggle with this. Take your time, dig deep and make sure you get 10 down.

Do this now.

Put this list somewhere safe.

These are your 'get out of psychological jail free' cards. You can now create what I call the 'happy hat'. In my hat I have an array of things I enjoy doing, nothing longer than half an hour. When I feel pressure mounting up I grab a lucky dip from the 'happy hat' and spend that time enjoying my life – guilt-free. I know that the time I spend there will make the time I spend on the more purposeful tasks more productive, more enjoyable and more effective.

Without meeting your own basic needs as depicted in Maslow's 'Hierarchy of Needs', you're about as useful as an ashtray on a motorbike.

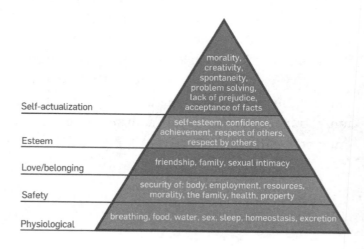

Self-actualization — morality, creativity, spontaneity, problem solving, lack of prejudice, acceptance of facts

Esteem — self-esteem, confidence, achievement, respect of others, respect by others

Love/belonging — friendship, family, sexual intimacy

Safety — security of: body, employment, resources, morality, the family, health, property

Physiological — breathing, food, water, sex, sleep, homeostasis, excretion

CHAPTER 19

Are you happy to be right or right to be happy?

All too often we find ourselves in the throes of a warm debate, of no value, with loved ones, friends and otherwise. I'm not taking myself out of the frame here; if anything, this once applied to me more than anyone I know. A statement was made once to me that stuck in my head and began a shift in my thinking. Upon seeing me grow uneasy over the lack of agreement on my seemingly logical point, a student interjected, "What does it really matter? Would you rather be right or be happy?"

The sentence stays with me to this day and many times I ask myself prior to opening a debate: *What is my intention here? Is it to be right or to be happy?* I've never before proved someone wrong to then be told how grateful they are and that I'm the man and my ego deserves a stroke. More often than not I have found that what had been a sound relationship became tense and unsettled.

My first step in hearing a point I disagree with now is to enquire further. I operate from a standpoint that this person has had experience that has led them to this belief – and I am able to learn something. I open my imagination to the idea that maybe, just maybe, they know something I don't and maybe if I ask them with integrity they might share it with me. Einstein once said that 'imagination is more important than knowledge because knowledge is limited to what we now know and imagination opens doors to new thinking.'

There are many bonuses to seeking to understand from the very beginning: first, there's the opportunity to learn things you don't already know; second, you manage to maintain a better level of rapport and engagement within your relationships and daily communications. If you enter any discussion (whether a negotiation, conversation or disagreement) with this in mind – to seek first to understand rather than to be understood – your potential to exit with a positive outcome is drastically multiplied.

It's absolutely possible that even once you have heard someone out, you still will not agree with them. That's fine; it is your right. What you will gain in spite of your disagreement is a better understanding of why they think as they do, how to move forward and a better connection with that person. They'll feel happier at least on an unconscious level that you heard them out.

Without exception, everyone likes to be heard and understood. All too often we power through the opinions and thoughts of others in a bid to convey our own. You learn by listening and not by talking.

EARLY TO RISE
MAKES A MAN HEALTHY
WEALTHY AND WISE

- BENJAMIN FRANKLIN

CHAPTER 20

Get more for your 24

We've all fallen prey at some point to the excuse that there aren't enough hours in a day. There aren't enough days in a week, weeks in a month, months in a year and so forth. What would you say if I told you that *I've found them*?

Controversial as this chapter may be, I believe that there is a direct correlation between sleep and success. Having looked at successful people like Sir Richard Branson, I found that many are members of the elite 5am Club who begin their day at 5 in the morning. On finding this out a few years back I decided it was only right that I joined the club too. Not many people are up at 5. It's a bit of an unsociable hour. Perfect – *no distractions*. Within just a few weeks my life had transformed.

After I get up (waking to an app that matches my circadian rhythms) I head to the kitchen and consume a blend of nutrients coupled with a glass of water with a pinch of Himalayan rock salt added to alkalise the body and replace fluid that I may have lost overnight. The body is a complex machine – look after it!

Shortly after 5 o'clock I begin on my self-development. This can comprise a number of additional things but will always include 30 minutes of reading, 15 minutes on my Daily Reflections (which are available to download for free on the www.burnthebullshit.com website), and at least 15 minutes that I spend planning my day with my goals in mind, setting 3 clear targets for that day.

That takes me to 6 o'clock. At 6 o'clock I train – weights, running or some form of hybrid training. I like to get training done in the morning for a number of reasons: I can't later get side tracked and miss a session, it sets me up mentally for the day and it also kick-starts my metabolism for the day. The benefits are endless. By the time I am done with these initial two phases of my morning routine I'm firing on all cylinders both mentally and physically, while most people are still only just getting out of bed.

So, why do I tell you all of this? Let's talk a little bit about sleep. How much sleep should we have? Well, 'scientists say' (and my Nan too) that we should have 8 hours of sleep every night. That theory is fine, I used to use that excuse too. Previously when waking up tired I didn't realise that I was in fact oversleeping – I even thought that it was because I was under rested and overslept more. Have you ever had a day where you had a long sleep and then woke up feeling groggy? Perhaps so much so that you struggled to snap out of that state for the rest of the day?

Some of you don't want to succeed as much as you want to sleep – Eric Thomas

I mentioned earlier that I looked at how much people were sleeping. I looked at Arnold Schwarzenegger. As discussed he's an extremely successful man in a number of categories. He said in his 2009 Commencement Address at University of California that he sleeps 6 hours a night: "There are 24 hours in a day. You sleep six hours and have 18 hours left. Now, I know there are some of you out there that say well, wait a minute, I sleep eight hours or nine hours. Well then, just sleep faster, I would recommend."

Now here is a man (a big one at that) who is advocating sleeping for 6 hours and delivering consistently great results in his life. He pretty much blew my 'needing extra sleep because I train a lot' excuse out of the water, world champion body builder that he is! My personal findings after sleeping an average of 5 hours and 40 minutes a night over the space of 90 nights were (amongst other things) that I had more energy, a better body, greater results within my business, was studying more, felt more focused and, I would go so far as to say, got a real sense of personal gratification.

What time you can get yourself out of bed is a reflection of your mindset. If you conquer that urge to sleep then you can conquer anything – *how you do one thing is how you do everything.* That means if you can succeed with regulating your sleep, then you can succeed with regulating your diet, and you can succeed with regulating your work and your life.

I once dismissed an employee because I found out that she was being dishonest with her spouse about smoking. She had told him that she quit a year ago but was consistently still smoking around 10 death sticks a day. Legalities of the dismissal aside you may say it sounds trivial. Is it really trivial when you consider that this person's spouse should be the person for whom she held the highest respect and yet she was lying to him?

If people can lie to their spouses, what would they do to us? She lacked integrity and one of the core values of the company is congruence, walking our talk. If you want to know what someone is really like, take a look at how they treat the ones they claim to love and you'll get an idea of what they have in store for you. As I said, *how we do one thing is how we do everything.*

Okay here's the exciting part: maths! If **Person A** sleeps 8 hours a night and **Person B** sleeps 6 hours a night, then there's a 2 hour difference in how long they're asleep. What that means is that there's a 2 hour difference in how long they're awake. Now, let's multiply that across the year. 2 hours, every single day, 365 days a year equates to 730 hours of sleep. 730 extra hours **Person B** gets to be awake every year. That means **Person B** gets an additional 45 of **Person A's** 16 hour days every year! An extra month and a half! Compared to **Person A, Person B** is alive for 13 and a half months every year!

I honestly think that if you have the audacity to claim that you've got dreams, visions, beliefs, aspirations – and you're sleeping on them – then you don't want them bad enough. Simple.

CHAPTER CHALLENGE

MIND OVER MATTRESS

I challenge you to try the 5am Club on for size. If you work night shifts or have a schedule that doesn't permit this, then exercise a degree of common sense and adapt the plan to suit your needs. The key thing I am challenging you to do is not so much get up at 5am; it is to stop oversleeping. Drop the bullshit excuse that you need 8 hours and try 6.

Try sleeping 6 undisturbed hours a night for a period of at least 21 days. Notice a recurrent theme with the number of days? According to Dr Maltz, author of Psycho-Cybernetics, it takes '21 days for an old mental image to dissolve and a new one to gel.' The journey of a lifetime starts with just 1 day. Make it happen!

CHAPTER 21

Media Madness

Modern culture is riddled with negativity and reeks of the bullshit that we are all subjected to on a daily basis. In an interview with ITV, I was once asked what I thought was the worst show on television. Without hesitation I replied: 'the news'. It's a no-brainer for me; we are constantly fed doom and gloom on the newsreels and we swallow it all, hook, line and sinker. If it isn't about more financial turmoil on the horizon, then it's about criminality, sexual deviancy or some form of passive-aggressive hate mongering. This is just as much the case with newspapers and radio as it is with television.

People find it incredibly easy to buy into media bullshit without much critical evaluation of what is being presented. It is sad that so many otherwise intelligent people are susceptible to these influences. The implication is, 'oh it's in the paper, which means it must be true'. Despite the fact we all know how biased and false some of the media stories can be, we still happily assume opinions, regurgitate unverified 'facts' and act in accordance with what we are told. Our instinct for survival means we have an innate fear of existential threats; the tabloids in particular play on this to boost their audiences. Their hooks are primed for us with worms of fear.

For example, you could be forgiven for thinking nowadays that we are all under constant threat of attack from Islamic extremists from the constant fear mongering in the media. Given that Islam is a religion that proclaims 'love for all, hatred for none', the danger must come from only a small minority of extremists, yet terrorism is often linked with Islam in a way that means all members of that religion are scapegoated.

Note also the fantastic power of the word 'terrorist', a word that instantly grabs your attention. According to an analysis by the New America Foundation, terrorist attacks in the United States have led to the deaths of 45 people since the shocking atrocity of 9/11, an average of 3.2 a year since 2001. In the UK David Anderson QC, independent reviewer of Terrorism Legislation, reported in 2010 that the average annual death toll in the UK due to terrorism was just 5. Of course even one such death is too many and it is an absolute tragedy that people become victims of political terror but the point here is that the overwhelming fear of Islamic extremism is disproportionate to the reality of the threat.

To put it into perspective, in the UK 29 people died from drowning in the bathtub in one year alone - yet I don't see any campaigns to make people wear snorkels in the bath! You are literally more likely to get struck by lightning than to be a terror victim. Studies show that 49 people a year die in the USA from lightning strikes. That means you are 15 times more likely to be fatally struck by lightning than to die at the hands of violent extremists!

Conveniently the tabloids give less prominence to the enormous number of lives lost every year to self-inflicted illnesses resulting from smoking, drinking or poor diet.

Strange that none of these are a 'code red' and people are still allowed to buy their death-sticks and sugary treats over the counter. Unfortunately for us the government is tied to business and not as benevolent as we are usually led to believe.

That isn't a problem because the last time I checked I am a grown-up, able to look after myself and make my own decisions. My point is that we should not seek to be mollycoddled to stop us killing ourselves and others, but that we should take responsibility for our own lives and be more than mere pawns in someone else's chess game.

I have not read a newspaper for years and, believe it or not, my business, social life and intelligence have certainly not suffered as a result. A friend told me once that 'if there is anything that you really need to know, someone will tell you' and I do pick up snippets of news and information in this way. But when people ask me 'don't you think you should show more of an interest in what is going on in the world?' I say, 'yes, but I'm a great deal more interested in what I can do in the world'.

I certainly know enough to get moving and I don't see the point in worrying about things over which I have zero control or influence. I would sooner read a book or watch a documentary with some direct relevance to my life and with no secret political or commercial agenda.

Media is just one side of the coin; the other is 'entertainment'. Soap operas are the biggest, most negative, brain-polluting crock of bullshit around. Take your average TV soap. The storyline usually revolves around something negative like stealing, petty backstabbing or infidelity or take your pick from a whole host of other anti-social themes. Is this really what we enjoy watching? Consider the effect this has on your brain, this constant conditioning for negativity. Why warp your vision and appreciation of the world you live in and become paranoid that everyone is going to let you down or hurt you in some way?

The truth is that there are multitudes of positive, supportive, constructive, contributing, monogamous, integral and all-round nice people in this world. I have had the pleasure of meeting plenty of them throughout my life. Fortunately the type of work I do also tends to attract the 'right' type of person. Would fictional representatives of this type of person make good TV? I guess not. Hence I do not watch much TV although I must confess to having appeared on it from time to time.

How many hours do you think people spend watching TV? In Britain, the average person watched more than 4 hours of television every day in 2011. Over the entire year, that amounts to 1460 hours viewing. Add this brain-deadening waste of time to the time you spend 'oversleeping' and you will soon find the extra hours you need to take your life to the next level and beyond.

Imagine the difference that just four extra hours a day could make to your overall quality of life, health and happiness, if just one of those hours was spent exercising, one was spent reading or learning and the remaining two were spent as quality time with a loved one, friend or, just as importantly, in private reflection. Note the emphasis here is on quality; sitting watching the television is not quality time. Having a discussion, learning something real, looking into someone's eyes and adding value to someone's life, THAT is real quality time. What could you use your extra time for?

CHAPTER CHALLENGE
DIGITAL DETOX

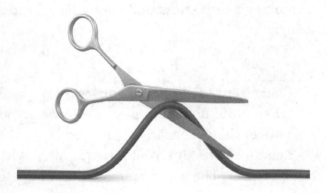

My challenge to you is this: bin the TV, ditch the newspapers and switch off the radio.

Do this for 21 days from today.

If you are serious about eradicating bullshit from your life and want to achieve a life of freedom and happiness you must first detox your brain. Work out what you will substitute for the wasteful habits in advance so that you don't get caught out with idle time and fall back into the bad habits.

It's no wonder that we have the saying 'the

Devil finds work for idle hands' because we are tempted to fill idle time with negative, destructive activities such as watching bullshit TV, smoking death sticks and eating legal crack; aka sugar.

- Cancel any newspaper subscriptions and when you do walk past a News stand notice how negative or useless the headlines are 'Jim from X Factor slept with his cat' or 'The war on terror continues' etc

- Ban radio - instead download or purchase audiobooks of value, maybe learn a foreign language. For music, listen to downloads or CDs

- Totally disconnect the TV from the mains. You do not need it

- Avoid online newsfeeds like the plague

- Accumulate positive, varied, educational literature and read it

- Write a list of at least 10 things you could spend your time doing that will give you greater (short or long term) benefit than watching TV and do them

- Keep a log of the extra things you get done and the effects on you of these measures. Use this material to recap and assess progress at the end

CHAPTER 22

Time you enjoy wasting is not time wasted

Your life is as good as the emotions you experience on a day-to-day basis and the emotions you inspire in others. With this in mind, you should not be causing yourself stress or discomfort worrying about the prospect of becoming successful, when, as we now know, success itself is a state of mind that you can have straight away. It is all too easy in today's fast paced society to be 'working on your dream,' all the while forgetting to live it.

I will happily smash a 15 hour day in the office several days in a row but I also love a long walk in the countryside on a summer's day or hanging with friends with no time constraints and no agenda. And when I am with someone, I really am *with* that person and that person alone, which means no phones in sight. What we are referring to here is not being idle or lazy; it's being balanced.

There are copious benefits that come with leading a balanced life, such as the fact that happiness is in the now and not something to be deferred. All the while you are deferring happiness you are in fact conditioning the mind to not experience it. Your brain is like a muscle; condition that muscle for happiness and you will experience it stronger, more intensely and more readily than ever before.

Another important thing to be careful of is burning out. It's all good smashing work (especially when you are enjoying it), but neglect your social life, spouse, health or family and you will pay heavily in the long run. It's all too easy to say that you will allow yourself more time to relax when x happens at work or y happens to your bank balance.

That's great but when you burn out, get ill or lose your autonomy (and in turn the love for what you do), then this will be reflected in your ability to work and thus negatively impact the output of your work. Stress overload will cause the most resilient, most durable and most able to crash and burn.

Stress is the root of most illness; disease itself is essentially the amalgamation of the words *dis-ease*, therefore implying that there is some kind of dis-ease or unrest within the body. The mind and body is a totally linked system, the 'mind' by definition essentially existing throughout the body. Often misquoted when referring to the brain, which is an organ, the mind is our neurological structure in its entirety. While there are many illnesses brought on by stress that we could list here, it would suffice to say that avoiding unhealthy levels of stress is ideal.

So, what do you do to ensure balance?

If you are going to do something then do something well, if you are going to do nothing, then do nothing well.

Confused? What I am saying is this: when you are working, then work, don't fritter time and attention away wishing that you were relaxing. By the same token, when you are relaxing, *relax*. Don't sit and feel guilty for not being at work and then fail to give your relaxation time proper attention.

***

We wrestle so many inner conflicts on a daily basis it can make it hard to progress in any area, and when we do it makes our progress hard to measure. The magic trick is integrating the different demands on your time that are driving you in seemingly opposite directions. Balance them, know that you have all of them attended to and make sure that when you are doing one of them, you will do it well. This means not feeling guilty on holiday but allowing yourself to feel totally immersed; not feeling distant when working but totally present and committed.

This can take a degree of planning. By organising your schedule in advance you can look and know that you have all bases covered, which will then stop you having to think about it midway through a romantic meal.

Take for example, a student with an upcoming exam. His friends are out on Saturday and he has a project to complete for Monday.

Now he could stay in and work whilst wishing he was out or he could go out and feel bad for not working. Neither answer is conducive to a state of happiness. The trick then lies in planning and *deciding*. Making the decision to allocate the time on the Sunday so that the Saturday can be enjoyed guilt free.

Decision is a word derived from Latin meaning to 'cut away from.' So, once you have your decision, for it to truly be a decision by definition you have *cut away from* all other options. Decide what it is you are going to do and then, when it's time, do it well, no distractions. If you are going to have a well-deserved night watching bad movies, chilling out with your better half and eating a pizza then *do it well*! Don't moan about calories; one bad meal is not going to make you fat as much as one good meal will not make you thin. Time you enjoy wasting is absolutely, categorically, definitely, unquestionably *not* time wasted, so waste your time wisely.

A TEACHER AFFECTS ETERNITY;
HE CAN NEVER TELL WHERE
HIS INFLUENCE STOPS.
HENRY ADAMS

CHAPTER 23

Be the change

If you want something, you have to **be** that thing. Mahatma Gandhi said that you should *be the change that you want to see in the world*. Don't ask for the change, **be the change**. Congruence is the true measure of an individual. It's of paramount importance that you exemplify what you want to see in the world and that you are what you say you are and practice what you preach. You have to walk the walk, as well as talk the talk. People won't buy into you if you don't walk the walk.

If you want the perfect partner, then **be** the perfect partner. If you want the perfect business, then **be** the perfect businessman. Don't expect what you're not willing to project. It isn't the money but the person you become in order to make the money that is key. I don't know anyone who's made a lot of money from scratch who is overly worried about losing it all. A true entrepreneurial character can make it 100 times over.

I have had the personal experience of facing the loss of the entirety of my funds, assets and career – my entire life's work. I also had an occasion in the past when a considerably large sum of money was stolen from me. On neither of these occasions did I lose heart or take it personally. Instead, I made use of it both as an opportunity to grow as a human being and a businessman.

The first time that I faced losing everything, property, car, money, I stopped to ask why I didn't let it get to me. I realised that it was simple – I could just make it all again, and it was merely one more challenge I had to face in my life. In fact, when I look back now, it was fun making it again. I wasn't worried because I knew how I'd made it in the first place and more importantly I knew who I had been.

I had a slight disagreement with my father at the time of the first near loss and when I explained the situation to him he was very understandably worried. I was sat on the sofa across from him as he deliberated the prospect of his 24 year old son being wiped out financially. 'It's not the end of the world,' I replied, 'It's just money, I can make some more, I'm only young.' Thus the debate ensued.

In hindsight, I appreciate the difference in perspective; my father was born into less favourable finances and the prospect of losing such considerable security was potentially the difference between eating and starving. Following his father passing away, my dad was tasked with working to support his mother and later on his brother who suffered a mental breakdown and serious disability.

Although I wasn't raised in luxury either, I was raised in an era of opportunity. I was blessed to grow up on the wave of a dynamic and entrepreneurial epoch where making money was a case of will, creativity and action and not only reserved for those with a glowing CV and array of qualifications.

Life is a game. You're not going to get out of the game alive. There are no 'continues' or extra lives, so don't be afraid for your funds and your finances to fluctuate, just play the game and see what you can get out of it. Having that frame of mind prevents you emotionally attaching yourself to money (not in a negative way anyway). It's fun when it's fun and when it's not fun it's a challenge, which is fun in itself. Every single occurrence or event has only the meaning that you place on it so choose your meanings with care.

***

Remember that who you are literally changes the world. I don't speak with exaggeration, I do mean literally. Just a smile alone can change the destiny of a stranger. Consider this: in 2013 6,233 people in the UK committed suicide - that corresponds to a rate of 11.9 people per 100,000. These are people that you pass on the street, that serve you in a shop, that sit next to you on a train. What if you could lift someone's spirits on a certain day just enough to save their life, what if you could influence someone just at the right time to make that critical difference?

Even if that stranger is not on the edge of taking their own life, you can still add phenomenal value to the quality of their life. Just a smile and a simple hello can change someone's day for the better and impact all their subsequent interactions. Remember that every move you make inspires others in some way because we continually learn from one other. Together we can make this floating rock a better place for all.

The core message of this book is not to moan about what is wrong but to take ownership and make it right. To free yourself from the bullshit, unlock your potential, and ultimately achieve the life that you deserve.

Let the change begin with you.

CHAPTER CHALLENGE

COMPETENCE IN CONFIDENCE

You don't get what you want out of life – you get who you are, what you share and who you spend time with.

Develop a circle of peers around you who encourage confidence by highlighting competence. Make a habit of telling each other what you think you each do well.

Tell yourself 3 things that you think you do well every day. Partner up with a friend, family member, spouse or colleague and tell them three things you think they do well every day, and get them to do the same.

This practice both reinforces your confidence and also helps you to notice how great the people around you are whilst strengthening theirs.

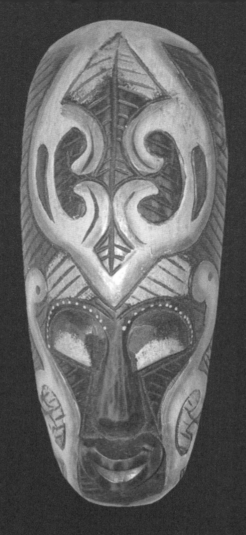

IF THERE IS NO ENEMY WITHIN
THEN THE ENEMY OUTSIDE
CAN DO YOU NO HARM
AFRICAN PROVERB

IT'S TIME

LET'S BURN SOME BULLSHIT

Are you ready to burn your bullshit?

First, get into a strong and powerful state. Use the skills and techniques you have picked up so far in this book. Utilise your physiology – pump yourself up and then sit up straight in your chair with a sense of purpose. Perhaps play some music in the background throughout this exercise that makes you feel strong and capable. Repeat an empowering mantra until you are ready and then grab your pen and paper with calm determination.

Next consider **three** pivotal bullshit beliefs you are carrying around. Choose ones that you know are holding you back. Think specifically about how they have stopped you in the *past*, how they are stopping you *now* and how they will stop you in the *future* if you don't burn and eradicate them.

If carrying these bullshit beliefs with you is stifling your dreams then what is the alternative to burning them *now*? Are you prepared to take your goals, aspirations and passions to the grave with you? Are you prepared to die unsatisfied and unfulfilled? If not then *now* is the time.

The saddest thing about walking through a graveyard is not the dead bodies but the dead ambitions. The things that we as people did not get to see, hear and enjoy because somebody was too scared to show us. The inventions that never made the light, the songs that were never sung, the love that was never expressed or the potential that was never realised. Bullshit beliefs killed their vision – don't let your bullshit kill yours. Would you rather live in belief or die in fear?

Now write down three bullshit beliefs that have been doing their best to hold you back

For example:

- I *don't have* the knowledge to run my own business

Once you have three bullshit beliefs listed spend five minutes on each one explaining in as many words as possible what's ridiculous about holding such a belief – why it's bullshit. Why would someone else think it is bullshit? What would your true friends say about it? What would I say (bearing in mind I wrote the book on the stuff)? What have these limiting beliefs prevented you from achieving? What will getting rid of them allow you to do?

Write fast, write decisively – as long as you get something down. *Anything.* Don't worry too much about spelling, no one else is going to see what you've written!

Now the time has come to cast off your old shackles and start afresh – safely take the list with the bullshit on it and do to that list what it has been doing to you for the past who knows how long, burn it. Yes, actually light it up! Dispose of it. Do it now, do it carefully, do it supervised and above all safely but do it. If you would prefer to rip it up then fine, rip it into a thousand pieces. Make it dramatic. Screw the paper up and throw it against the wall.

Obliterate those old beliefs and as you do, talk to them. Let them know that **you** are the one in charge now. Make sure you destroy them so that absolutely, categorically, no matter what, **they are never coming back**.

Feel good? Feel strong? Feel in charge?

Good. Next, on a new sheet of paper, list three positive, new and empowering beliefs that you are going to replace the bullshit ones with. Think big. Stretch the imagination without stretching the truth. You don't have to accept these straight away but as Les Brown says, 'it's good just to realise and accept the fact that *it's possible.*'

For example:

- I have the skills, resources and capabilities to learn all that I need to know about starting a business

Last but not least, I want you to list the reasons why you believe these new statements to be true. Spend five minutes on each one. This is it – you are finally beginning on the road to the life you deserve. Sit up tall and feel good!

How you physically perform this step will influence the process. Pour out as many reasons as you can in support of your new and empowering beliefs. Consider what doors these new beliefs will open for you? What opportunities? What dreams? What aspirations? How will having these new beliefs make you feel? How does having these new beliefs make you feel? How **do** you feel?

Do this *now*.

Take these beliefs, make them look pretty and stick them somewhere you will see them every day. Stick them everywhere. Stick them anywhere. Read and repeat them until you understand that this is, has always been and will always be the truth. Share them. Embody them. This is what you really deserve, not that bullshit that held you back. This is what you **can** do, what you **will** do and what you **must** do.

Allow me to be the first to congratulate you on setting yourself free, on completing this book, on walking your walk, on resolving to be the best you can be and most of all on burning your bullshit. I wish you every success in the future and don't forget to share your stories, strengths and strategies with those who you meet along the journey of your life. Only by helping others to reach their potential can we ever truly expect to reach our own.

Live appreciatively, live generously, live completely, live passionately and of course 'Live Daily'.

Chapter Summaries

Congratulations! You have made it through. You truly are one of the few that does. Allow me to personally wish you the best for your future. Before I leave you to enjoy your new life let's quickly review the key points from each chapter.

1. **You'd better believe it**

    Beliefs can be split into two types: empowering and disempowering. Beliefs inspire behaviour which in turn produces results. Every belief, and every subsequent action, has a positive intention, but we must question whether it is serving us well.

2. **The seeds of all bullshit**

    We often hold onto beliefs for years due to confirmation bias, which preserves an instilled belief. We don't update these beliefs due to fear. We get stuck in the same routines and same habits and don't grow.

3. **What happened?**

   A lot of our beliefs were instilled in us as children. Often education can leave us with knowledge but the inability to apply it. It is your responsibility to change your own life. In order to have something, you must act.

4. **Bullshit goes in, bullshit comes out** We receive information through our 5 senses. All this information is filtered – our senses are limited and we do not fully experience the world. We can also only process a small amount of information at a time, leaving our view of the world even more restricted. For this reason, we should focus on the good.

5. **What do you think of that?**

   Once we have received the raw data, we then interpret it and place our own meanings on it. We often misinterpret information due to biases and filters.

6. **Creature vs Creator**

    You can either be a creature of circumstance, where things happen to you, or a creator of circumstance, where you make things happen. A creature will place blame on outside influences, a creator knows that it is all their own doing. Creators believe in themselves, despite external factors that may be seen to hold them back.

7. **If you can see it, you can be it**

    Recognise a quality or behaviour you would like, and become it through modelling it.

8. **Body language of a champion**

    You can influence your mood by utilising your body. Consciously adopt a physiology and tonality that best suits how you want to feel.

9. **Spoilt for choice**

    There is always a choice, in how we feel and how we choose to respond. We always have some element of control over the external world. We do not react to events but rather to the meaning we place upon them. You can reframe a positive meaning onto any event if you choose to.

10. **Life balance over bank balance**
Money should not define your life. Your quality of life should be determined based on the quality of your emotions. Clarify what finances you require, but ensure you are enjoying the life you have now.

11. **So what do you want? And how much of it?**
In setting goals, it is important not to focus on the negative, but state it in the positive. When we try not to do something, we inevitably focus on it, and as such do just that.

12. **F.E.A.R: False Evidence Appearing Real**
    We only have two innate fears from birth, and the rest are inherited throughout our lives, with most tracing back to fear of being rejected and fear of not being good enough. You can choose to label something as fear, or as excitement, as both have the same physiological responses.

13. **Smokescreens**
    We often misinterpret our emotions and blame them on something else. Being clear on our values helps to align our goals and ensure we are working towards the correct ones.

14. **The 'but' flip**
    Changing a sentence from 'x but y' to 'y but x because z' allows us power to choose, and avoids bullshit excuses.

15. Honesty over modesty

We often use the term 'humble' incorrectly, and similarly label confidence as arrogance; arrogance is when confidence is miscommunicated. Be confident and encourage that same confidence in others.

16. Have you got crabs?

The crab bucket mentality exists where people pull others down where they are becoming successful. Do not let others doubt you or hold you back, and be careful not to be a crab yourself. Jealousy is a waste of our energy. You are jealous when you recognise something you want yourself. Instead of being jealous, model the behaviour, and use the emotion as a trigger to act.

17. Good for nothing

Being good for nothing, with no expectation of reward, is a true measurement of an individual's greatness. Give freely, with no expectation. This is where you will experience true happiness.

18. **You have to be selfish to be selfless**
You must look after yourself first before you can help others. To truly help others we must be in a peak performance state, so self-care is essential.

19. **Are you happy to be right or right to be happy?**
You do not always need to be right. Respect others opinions, and accept their opinions even if you choose not to agree with them.

20. **Get more for your 24**
There is often seen to be a direct correlation between sleep and success. Get more time from your day by sleeping less.

21. **Media Madness**

The media offers us a distorted view on the world. You are more likely to die from being struck by lightning than a terrorist attack, despite the fear mongering portrayed in the media. Challenge yourself to not watch any TV or listen to radio for 21 days.

22. **Time you enjoy wasting is not wasted time**

It is important to ensure you do not burn out. Stress is a root cause of most illness. Do everything well, including doing nothing.

23. **Be the Change**

If you want something, you have to be that thing. Be the change you wish to see.

Notes

You'd better believe it

William Shakespeare, *Hamlet,* (2006)

Robert L Leahy, *The Worry Cure: Seven Steps to Stop Worry from Stopping You*, (2005)

The seeds of all bullshit

Robin Sharma, *The Monk who sold his Ferrari,* (1997)

Sigmund Freud, quoted within "The Place of Actions in Personality Change" by Allen Wheelis, Psychiatry, (1950 May)

Michael Shermer, *The Believing Brain: From Spiritual Faiths to Political Convictions – How We Construct Beliefs and Reinforce Them as Truths,* (2012)

Deepak Chopra, *Quantum Healing*, (1989)

What happened?

Tom Bodett, *The End of the Road,* (1987)

Taken from Arnold Schwarzenegger, USC Commencement address (2009) available at www.usc.edu

Bullshit goes in, bullshit comes out

Dr. Wayne W Dyer, *The Power of Intention,* (2005)

George Miller, *"The Magical Number Seven, Plus or Minus Two: Some Limits on Our Capacity for*

Processing Information" Psychological Review 63 (2), (1956)

Maurice DeCastro, *Hamster to Harmony: Get Off the Wheel and Live your Best Life!* (2009)

What do you think of that?

Tupac Shakur, "So Many Tears"

Derek Landy, *Skullduggery Pleasant: Death Bringer,* (2011)

Creature vs Creator

Frederick Nietzsche, *Twilight of the Idols or, How to Philosophize with a Hammer,* (1889)

Body language of a champion

Albert Mehrabian, *Silent Messages,* (1971)

Robert Zajonic, Murphy, Shelia T, IngleharT, Marita, "*Feeling and Facial Efference:*

Implications of the Vascular Theory of Emotion", Psychological Review 96 (3), (1989)

Amy Cuddy, Caroline A Wilmuth and Dana R Carne, *"The Benefit of Power Posing Before a High Stakes Social Evaluation"*, Harvard Business School Working Paper, No 13-127, (2012)

Amy Cuddy, *Your body language shapes who you are,* available from http://ted.com

Spoilt for choice

Standard common law test for criminal liability

Taken from Buddhaghosa, *Visuddhimagga,* (approx. 430 CE)

Stephen Covey, *The 7 habits of highly effective people*, (1989)

F.E.A.R. False Evidence Appearing Real

Wayne Dyer, *The Power Of Intention: Change The Way You Look At Things And The Things You*

Look At Will Change: Learning to Co-Create Your World Your Way, (2004)

Rene Descartes, Meditations on First Philosophy, (1641)

Byron Katie, The Work, available from thework.com/en

Smokescreens

Sigmund Freud, *"On the grounds for detaching a particular syndrome from neurasthenia under the description "anxiety neurosis"",* (1894)

The Disney creative strategy

As explained by Robert Dilts, *Walt Disney, Strategy of a Genius,* (1994)

Have you got crabs?

Drake, from "Over my Dead Body"

Good for nothing

Ken Blanchard, *Whale Done!: The Power of Positive Relationships,* (2003)

Media Madness

Data from New America Foundation available at: http://securitydata.newamerica.net/extremists /deadly-attacks.html

Data from National Oceanic and Atmospheric Administration available at: http://www.lightningsafety.noaa.gov/fatalities. shtml

From BARB, available at: http://www.barb.co.uk/whats-new/weekly- viewing-summary

Be the change

Data from Samaritans – 'Suicide statistics report 2015'

About the Author

Stephen Doran has written many published articles and is an official blogger for The Huffington Post. He has appeared on television on BBC's 'Special Forces - Ultimate Hell Week' and is on Dave channel's investment show, 'The Money Pit' where he is one of the key investors. He is well known for his many YouTube videos promoting the 'Live Daily' theme and for his powerful tips and techniques on how to lead a fulfilling life of contribution and achievement.

After growing up in South East London, Stephen left school and undertook various jobs before qualifying as a Firefighter at the tender age of eighteen. Seven years into that career he decided to become his own boss and left to develop his own business portfolio. To date he has created and managed several successful businesses including a Laser Clinic, a Mixed Martial Arts company, a cabaret event and more recently the 'Peak Performance Academy' a venture close to his heart and based on his personal approach to life.

Stephen's formula for success combines physical fitness with a positive mental outlook underpinned with unwavering self-belief. As an award winning after dinner speaker, he regularly delivers keynote talks and training workshops in global companies and universities, runs his own accredited PPA training courses and teaches subjects such as Public Speaking, Confidence and the 'Psychology of Success'. His energies are nowadays focused on the Personal/Professional Development industry where he aims to help others develop happy lives and achieve their goals.

BURN THE BULLSH!T

www.burnthebullshit.com

Visit the website for FREE downloadable resources and worksheets that will allow you to continue to develop and progress your life

To have Stephen Doran speak at your organisation email **info@burnthebullshit.com**

Don't forget to check out the BURN THE BULLSHIT Audiobook, read by Stephen Doran

Follow Stephen on:

www.facebook.com/StephenMarkDoran

@officialstevedoran

www.twitter.com/officialsteved

www.YouTube.com/c/LiveDailyOfficial

We hope you enjoyed reading this book.

Your feedback and support is greatly appreciated, please go online at Amazon and leave a review.

I AM ALWAYS DOING THAT WHICH I CANNOT, IN ORDER THAT I CAN LEARN HOW TO DO IT.

PABLO PICASSO